CW00607296

Congratulations
on your Retirement!
May it be a long
and happy one!
Love Pete & Dawn
x x

Best walks in Yorkshire

Richard Sale

Best walks in Yorkshire

Constable · London

First published in Great Britain 1997
by Constable and Company Limited
3 The Lanchesters
162 Fulham Palace Road
London W6 9ER
Copyright © 1997 Richard Sale
The right of Richard Sale to be identified
as the author of this work has been asserted by him
in accordance with the
Copyright, Designs and Patents Act 1988
ISBN 0 09 476 350 X
Set in Palatino 9 pt by
CentraCet, Cambridge
Printed in Great Britain by
St Edmundsbury Press Ltd
Bury St Edmunds, Suffolk

A CIP catalogue record for this book
is available from the British Library

Contents

Illustrations   7
List of maps   9
Acknowledgements   11
Introduction   13
   Structure of the book   14
   Maps and mapping   15
   Mountain safety and the Country Code 16
   The walks graded according to difficulty 19
Yorkshire – a brief history   23

The Best Walks

THE YORKSHIRE DALES   33

  1: Cautley Spout   37
  2: Richmond   41
  3: Aysgarth Falls   49
  4: The Ingleton Waterfalls   57
  5: Hardraw Force   63
  6: The Three Peaks   71
     6a Pen-y-ghent   71
     6b Ingleborough   76
     6c Whernside   84
  7: Malham Cove and Gordale Scar   91
  8: Wharfedale and Littondale   103
  9: The Norber Erratics   109
10: Bolton Abbey and The Strid   115
11: How Stean Gorge   123
12: Swaledale and Tan Hill   129

THE NORTH YORK MOORS   137

13: Rievaulx   141
14: The Bride Stones   147
15: Roseberry Topping   153
16: Staithes and Runswick Bay   161
17: Rosedale   169
18: Goathland   175
19: Westerdale Moor   181
20: Osmotherley   191
21: Lilla Howe and Falling Foss   201
22: Whitby to Ravenscar   209

THE YORKSHIRE WOLDS   221

23: Wharram Percy   223
24: Millington Dale   227
25: Flamborough Head   233

THE VALE OF YORK   243

26: York   245
27: Fountains Abbey   255
28: Hovingham   263

THE PENNINES   269

29: Haworth   271
30: Pinhaw Beacon   281

Appendix 1: Other walks in Yorkshire   287
Appendix 1: Transport and weather   293
Appendix 3: Useful addresses   295

Index   299

Illustrations

THE YORKSHIRE DALES

Cautley Spout   38
Richmond Castle and the River Swale   45
Lower Force, Aysgarth   52
Pecca Falls   60
The stream below Hardraw Force   66
Pen-y-ghent from the south-west   72
Ingleborough from the east   80
The Ribblehead Viaduct and Whernside   88
Malham Cove   92
Drystone walls near Malham Cove   96
The entrance to Gordale Scar   100
Knipe Scar   106
A Norber Erratic   110
The Strid   118
Scar House Reservoir   126
The Tan Hill Inn   134

THE NORTH YORK MOORS

Rievaulx Abbey   142
Rievaulx Abbey   145
The Low Bride Stones   150
Captain Cook's Monument on Easby Moor   156
Rosebery Topping   159
Cowbar Nab, Staithes   164
Runswick Bay   167
Ruin beside the old Rosedale railway   172
The Roman road above Goathland   178

Young Ralph Cross   184
Fat Betty   188
The village cross and old barter table, Osmotherley   194
Mount Grace Priory   197
Oak Dale   198
The cross on Lilla Howe   206
Whitby   215
Robin Hood's Bay   216
Robin Hood's Bay from Boggle Hole   217

THE YORKSHIRE WOLDS

The ruined church, Wharram Percy   226
Millington Dale   230
The chalk tower, Flamborough Head   236
Selwicks Bay   238
The Fishermen's Memorial, Flamborough   241

THE VALE OF YORK

York Minster   250
The Shambles, York   252
The Studley Park Lake   256
Fountains Abbey   258
Fountains Abbey   261
The village green, Hovingham   266

THE PENNINES

Brontë Bridge   274
Top Withins   276
Porridge Stoop   282

List of maps

Map of Yorkshire   12

THE YORKSHIRE DALES

 1: Cautley Spout   36
 2: Richmond   42
 3: Aysgarth Falls   48
 4: The Ingleton Waterfalls   56
 5: Hardraw Force   64
 6a: Pen-y-ghent   70
 6b: Ingleborough   77
 6c: Whernside   85
 7: Malham Cove and Gordale Scar   90
 8: Wharfedale and Littondale   102
 9: The Norber Erratics   108
10: Bolton Abbey and The Strid   114
11: How Stean Gorge   122
12: Swaledale and Tan Hill   130

THE NORTH YORK MOORS

13: Rievaulx   140
14: The Bride Stones   148
15: Roseberry Topping   152
16: Staithes and Runswick Bay   160
17: Rosedale   168
18: Goathland   174
19: Westerdale Moor   182
20: Osmotherley   190
21: Lilla Howe and Falling Foss   202
22: Whitby to Ravenscar   210

THE YORKSHIRE WOLDS

23:   Wharram Percy   224
24:   Millington Dale   228
25:   Flamborough Head   234

THE VALE OF YORK

26:   York   244
27:   Fountains Abbey   254
28:   Hovingham   264

THE PENNINES

29:   Haworth   272
30:   Pinhaw Beacon   280

Acknowledgements

I would like to thank the staff of libraries throughout Yorkshire for their unfailing assistance during the research for parts of this book.

I thank Kate Bradbury, Robin Bradshaw and Susan Smith for their assistance on the routes, but most especially Mike Rogers for his companionship on many of the routes. His technical and personal criticism enlivened every mile.

All the photographs in the book were taken with Pentax camera equipment.

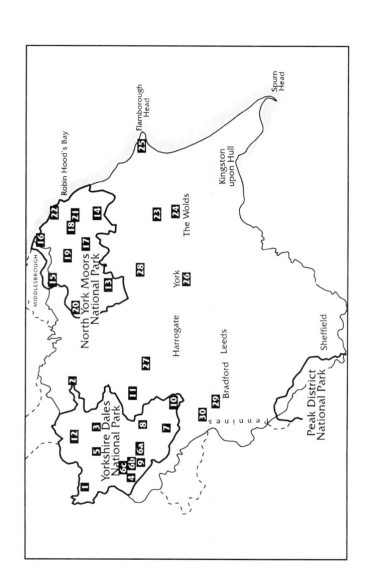

Introduction

This new volume of Best Walks uses the same selection criteria as were applied in previous volumes in the series. The thirty or so routes have therefore been selected to explore the variation of scenery that Yorkshire has to offer.

Yorkshire has an enviable position among the counties of England. Within its borders lie two National Parks – the Yorkshire Dales and North York Moors – a sea coast of varied interest, the Wolds and a good section of the Pennines, and towns of huge historical interest – York, Richmond, Harrogate. Though, as might be expected, the routes described concentrate on the National Parks, none of the country's features are ignored. The slight exception is the Pennines; the companion volume to the Peak District included a part of the south Pennines; so routes in that area of Yorkshire have been limited to two.

In exploring Yorkshire a decision had to be made on where exactly the county boundary lay. Was Yorkshire the old White Rose country or the newer version? A pragmatic view has been taken on this. The clear walking areas – the Dales, Moors, Wolds and Pennines – lie (more or less) within the confines of the new county boundaries. But if a route strays, then the wider view of what constitutes Yorkshire has been taken.

All but one of the routes are circular. The exception – the long coastal walk from Whitby to Ravenscar – has been included as a linear walk because to have 'bent' it would have been to sacrifice its character. Suggestions on return transport are made for this walk.

Finally, while every effort has been made to produce comprehensive and intelligible descriptions, and to back these up with equally clear maps, it must be emphasized that these should not be seen as anything but a supplement to possession of the maps mentioned at the start of each walk. Should you go off route, for whatever reason, only possession of the correct map will assist you back on to the correct line, or back to your transport.

Structure of the book
Because the area covered by the book is a large one, the walks have not been grouped together by category (see below for a definition of the walk categories) but by area. To help with a choice of route in the appropriate category, all the walks are given at the end of this introduction in increasing order of difficulty, i.e. the easiest first, the most difficult last.

Each of the areas is dealt with in a separate section, and the introduction to each section deals briefly with the particular historical, geographical or geological aspects of the area.

The walks have been divided into three categories, Easy, Intermediate and Difficult, the divisions making allowance not only for the time that a walk takes, but also for the terrain it crosses, and for the amount, and severity, of any climbing it involves. In broad terms, an Easy walk will take about two hours, an Intermediate walk up to twice as long, a good half-day's outing, while a Difficult walk will be, for most people, a long half-day's outing, or day's outing. As will be seen from the table of walks at the end of this introduction there are also a handful of walks that lie on the border between the categories. Those that lie between Easy and Intermediate are walks that cover easy ground, but take rather longer than other Easy walks, or ones that take the same time, but cover rather more difficult ground than those of the easier grade. In each case the walk does not really warrant the higher classification. The routes that lie between Intermediate and Difficult cover rough ground with few landmarks but are relatively short and flat.

The time given to each walk has been calculated using

Naismith's Formula, a well-known walking aid, which allows one hour for each 5 map-kilometres (3 map-miles) covered by an unladen walker and adds half an hour for each 300 m (1000 ft) of ascent. For most people this formula will under-estimate the time taken for a walk, and the under-estimation will increase as the time given for a walk increases. The reasons for this are several: firstly, no one will complete a walk in route-march style, but will pause occasionally to admire the view or watch the wildlife, and no allowance for these stops has been made; secondly, the formula makes no allowance for the roughness or otherwise of the terrain or for the effects of the weather; thirdly, no allowance has been made for rest stops, and these may be both more frequent and longer on the longer walks; and finally, the formula assumes that the walker can maintain his level of performance indefinitely. While some people can maintain 'Naismith' walking for many hours at a stretch many, especially those new to moorland walking, tire quickly and find not only that their rest stops increase and become longer but that they cover less ground while they are actually moving.

It is imperative, therefore, that the reader should use the walk-times as a guide only, and that newcomers to the area or to the sport should attempt lower-graded walks initially, and compare their actual performance with the given walk-time in order to gauge how long the more difficult walks will take them.

Maps and mapping

The relevant Landranger and Outdoor Leisure/Pathfinder Sheets are listed at the start of each walk. The walker is well served by Outdoor Leisure Sheets in Yorkshire, the Dales, Moors and south Pennines all being covered by that series.

Many of the walks described here are well trodden and signed and are not difficult to follow if the relevant map is carried. For these routes the maps merely indicate the line of conventional map signs. For some of the walks, however, the route finding is more complicated and the conventional map signs are supplemented by the following symbols:

```
Key:

ooooooooo    Intact wall          G     gate

 o o o o o   broken wall          K G   kissing gate

 +++++       fence or hedge        S    stile

 - - - - -   distinct path         L S  ladder stile

 .........   no path              -·-··  indistinct path

On all maps the following symbols are used:

  S          start point          ∎     feature of interest
```

Each map has a scale bar. They are drawn from personal observations, and so are not guaranteed to be absolutely to scale. Every effort has been made to ensure accuracy but from time to time walls and fences are erected or, more unusually, taken down. The author would be grateful for any information of such changes so that the book can be kept up to date.

Mountain safety and the Country Code

Though the upland areas of Yorkshire are low in comparison with the mountains of Wales, the Lake District and Scotland, they are real enough to a wet, cold and lost walker. That walker must be prepared for harsh conditions, particularly if he/she is out in winter.

Temperature decreases with altitude, the norm being a decrease of about 1°C every 150 m (about 2°C/300 ft) but it can be more in certain conditions. This means that the temperature on the summit of one of the Three Peaks could be as much as 5°C (9°F) lower than at the starting car-park. In addition, wind chill must be taken into account. Wind increases the convective heat loss from exposed skin, the wind chill temperature being the equivalent still-air temperature that would be required to produce the same heat loss, that is to 'feel as cold'. If the skin is wet, the chilling effect is further enhanced. It is not easy to give a simple rule of thumb for wind chill as the effect varies with air temperature and wind-speed, but as an example a 25 km per hour (15 m.p.h.) wind would reduce an air temperature of 10°C to an apparent temperature of about 2°C. Thus when the folk in the valley are enjoying a pleasant day with a temperature of around 20°C (68°C) the apparent temperature at the summit of one of the Three Peaks in a fresh wind would be around freezing.

These comments are not made to make the hills seem a playground for supermen, or to dissuade anyone from walking on them. It is just that it would be irresponsible not to warn any newcomer to mountain areas of the tricks they can play. Be prepared: if you have not done so already, get a copy of *Safety on Mountains*, a very small booklet from the British Mountaineering Council that tackles the very large subject of individual responsibility and safety.

It is also important that anyone contemplating expeditions into mountainous areas should be able to use a map and compass. If you are not familiar with these critical items, you could do no better than obtain a copy of Kevin Walker's *Mountain Navigation Techniques*, published in the same Constable series as this guidebook.

The majority of the walks in this book follow distinct paths. Please keep to them. The National Parks' only real pollution problem is people, and the cars that bring them. Under the sort of traffic some of the hills receive the laid pavements in town would groan after a few months. So, if on any of the walks the path is diverted to allow the ground to recover, or if there is a section of constructed pathway, be sympathetic to the problems. Of course it would be better if there were no obvious, scarring paths but the only really successful method of reducing wear to zero would be to ban all walkers.

THE COUNTRY CODE

The Code was prepared by the Countryside Commission with the help and advice of the many organizations concerned with the welfare of the countryside.

- Enjoy the country and respect its life and work
- Guard against all risk of fire
- Fasten all gates
- Keep dogs under close control
- Keep to public footpaths across all farmland
- Use gates and stiles to cross field boundaries
- Leave all livestock, machinery and crops alone
- Take your litter home
- Help to keep all water clean
- Protect wildlife, plants and trees
- Make no unnecessary noise

The walks graded according to difficulty

Name/Area/Number	Length in km	Ascent in metres	Time in hours	Terrain and Special Difficulties
EASY				
York Vale of York (26)	4.5	30	1.5	City walls and streets.
Rievaulx Moors (13)	4	45	1	Paths and lanes.
Wharram Percy Wolds (23)	4.5	90	1.5	Paths and lanes.
Bride Stones Moors (14)	4	70	1	Paths, some paved.
Cautley Spout	5	150	1.75	Paths. Steep and dangerous if the falls are approached.
Richmond Dales (2)	5.5	20	1.5	Paths and streets.
Ingleton Waterfalls Dales (4)	7	180	2.5	Paths and steps, some steep.
Fountains Abbey Vale of York (27)	7	70	1.5	Paths and lanes.
Hardraw Force Dales (5)	8	120	2	Paths and lanes.

EASY/INTERMEDIATE

Aysgarth Falls Dales (3)	6.5	50	2	Paths, some indistinct.
Hovingham Vale of York (28)	7.5	70	2	Paths and lanes. Forest section needs care.

INTERMEDIATE

Staithes and Runswick Bay Moors (16)	11	80	3	Path. Care needed on cliff edges.
Millington Wolds (24)	12	270	3.5	Paths and lanes.
Pinhaw Beacon South Pennines (30)	11	330	3.5	Paths. Moorland section weatherswept.
Wharfedale and Littondale Dales (8)	11	500	3.5	Paths. Considerable climbing in two sections.
Goathland Moors (18)	13	270	3.5	Paths. Section near Mallyan Spout is slippery.
Roseberry Topping Moors (15)	11	340	3	Paths and lanes.
Norber Erratics Dales (9)	11	375	3	Paths, some indistinct.

Osmotherley Moors (20)	14	280	3.5	Paths and lanes.
Haworth South Pennines (29)	14	275	4	Paths, some indistinct. Moorland section weatherswept.
Flamborough Head Wolds (25)	15	50	4	Paths and lanes. Cliff top sections need care.

INTERMEDIATE/DIFFICULT

Bolton Abbey and The Strid Dales (10)	12	50	3	Paths. Care needed approaching The Strid.
Malham Cove and Gordale Scar Dales (7)	11	200	3	Paths. Care needed in Gordale Scar and on limestone pavement, and with steep drops into the Cove.
Pen-y-ghent Dales (6a)	10.5	500	3	Paths. Considerable climbing and weatherswept.

DIFFICULT

Rosedale Moors (17)	12	300	3	Paths. High moor section weatherswept.
Westerdale Moors (19)	14	350	4	Paths. High moor section weatherswept.
How Stean Gorge Dales (11)	16	400	4	Paths and lanes.
Lilla Howe and Falling Foss Moors (21)	16	180	4	Paths, some indistinct. High section weatherswept.
Ingleborough Dales (6b)	12	600	4	Paths. Considerable climbing and weatherswept.
Whernside Dales (6c)	13	470	4	Paths. Considerable climbing and weatherswept.
Whitby to Ravenscar Moors (22)	20	280	5	Paths. Cliff edge sections need care.
Swaledale and Tan Hill Dales (12)	18	350	4.5	Paths and open, weatherswept moor.

Yorkshire – a brief history

As the ice retreated northwards at the end of the last Ice Age, around 8000 years ago, men followed it, perhaps to reoccupy areas that had supported their ancestors before the ice had forced them south. Of these hunter-gatherers there is no trace discernible to the untrained eye. Flints have been discovered in Yorkshire as elsewhere (most notably on Carlton Moor and near Burton Howe), finds that suggest a scattered, part-nomadic existence. Not until neolithic (New Stone Age) times, around 3000 BC, does man leave his mark on the landscape.

These first monuments are the long barrows. In their simplest form these were a 'box' of flat stones, three uprights and a capstone, which was then earthed over to form the long mound of the name. At many long barrows the covering earth has blown away, leaving the stones exposed. These are the cromlechs, or dolmens, that seep their way into local folklore, particularly in Celtic Britain – Wales and Cornwall. In later neolithic times more elaborate barrows were constructed, with side chambers leading from central passageways and false doorways (to confuse evil spirits or, perhaps, tomb robbers). It seems that Yorkshire's climate was harsher than that of southern Britain, for there are fewer long barrows here, and none of the craftsmanship and design of those found (for instance) on the Ridgeway.

The climate must have improved, however, for when Bronze Age folk replaced those of the neolithic era, they left behind ample evidence of their existence. The Bronze Age is characterized by the round barrow burial mound. Here the body of the deceased was cremated, the remains being laid below a circular mound of earth. The North York Moors areas especially has a number of such barrows, usually called 'howes' from the Danish word for a burial mound.

The folk raising the round barrows were also changing the landscape in more significant ways. The first was due to the change from a hunter-gatherer way of life to one based on farming, one of the two most profound revolutions in mankind's history. (Four thousand or so years later Yorkshire was also to play a significant part in the second, the Industrial Revolution.) The Agrarian Revolution was to alter the landscape for ever, clearing forests and draining marshes, a move from a wild to a 'managed' country.

The second change wrought by the round barrow builders was in the raising of megaliths. It is likely that the first megalith cultures arose in the late neolithic period, the use of standing stones, stone rows and circles for religious and ceremonial purposes (perhaps even as observatories and calendars) continuing into the Bronze Age. The stones, huge and enigmatic, have had a remarkable impact on later cultures, being incorporated into the legend and folklore of every community in which they stand. Yorkshire has nothing to compare with the monuments of Stonehenge and Avebury, but it does have some dramatic sites. At Rudston, to the west of Flamborough Head, stands the tallest stone in Britain. This vast monolith, almost 8 m (over 25 ft tall), is astonishing, not least for the sheer engineering effort of raising it. Equally dramatic are the Devil's Arrows – the name an indication of the awe in which megalithic sites were held by later cultures – near Boroughbridge, three huge stones (two are almost 7 m – actually 22 ft – tall, the other 5.5 m – 18 ft) erected in a north-south alignment. The stones are Millstone Grit, a very hard rock requiring a huge effort to cut, and were transported from Knaresborough, almost 10 km (6 miles) away.

When the Bronze Age gave way to the Iron Age it seems that Yorkshire's climate became colder and wetter. Certainly the high moorlands that had been popular with the barrow builders were abandoned in favour of lower lying, more sheltered areas. The most obvious feature left behind by the Iron Age cultures of Britain are the hill-forts, defensive encampments used to protect local populations during hostile incursions. The defences of the forts also indicate the sophistication of weapons. In their earliest form the forts were protected by a single ditch and rampart, adequate for attacks by spear-carrying invaders. Later, several ditches and ramparts were necessary to protect against the greater range of the sling shot, and elaborate gateways evolved, designed to turn an enemy's unprotected flank towards the fort's defenders. Britain's finest hill-forts are to be found in the south, Maiden Castle in Dorset being perhaps the finest of all, but Yorkshire does have examples. The fort on Ingleborough's summit enclosed an area of almost 15 acres, impressively large, but the most dramatic example is a coastal fort rather than a hill-fort, a ditch and rampart cutting off a headland, the sea providing adequate protection of the remaining sides. The ditch is Dane's Dyke, the headland Flamborough Head, this fine site being the focus of one of the walks described here (Walk 25). One further feature of Iron Age (Celtic) Britain is particularly found in Yorkshire, the square barrows of the Wolds. These barrows, constructed by the Parisi Celts, are rich in ornaments and weapons, the latter including dismantled chariots, and offer a unique picture of pre-Roman Yorkshire.

The Romans arrived in AD 43, the earlier 'invasion' by Julius Caesar having been little more than a reconnaissance. In the Roman Empire, York held a unique place as its northernmost town, one visited by several Emperors, including Hadrian (whose wall marked the actual northern frontier of the Empire) and Constantine. Before the coming of Rome York had been, if anything at all, a minor settlement. The Romans saw the advantages of a town where the Foss met the Ouse: this was the tidal limit of the Ouse, a river broad enough to take seagoing vessels. The Romans therefore chose it as their northern base, building Eboracum, a town whose ground plan can still be traced in modern York.

York was the headquarters of Legio IX Hispana, based here to subdue the Brigantes (the local Celts) and to protect southern Britain from incursions by the Picts. From York roads radiated out to other forts and, when the area had finally been pacified, settlements. There were signal stations on the coast from Filey to Huntcliff (though these were erected towards the end of Britain's Roman era), fortified camps at Virosidum, in Wensleydale, and Cawthorn, near Pickering (to name just two that have been excavated and are, therefore, well understood), and one of Britain's finest sections of Roman road can be seen on Wheeldale Moor. This remnant – part of a road that probably linked Cawthorn and the coast – is called Wade's Causeway after a local giant, and is visited on one of the walks described here (Walk 18).

By the 4th century AD York had become the provincial capital of Britannia Secunda, that section of the country between Hadrian's Wall and the estuaries of the Humber and the Mersey. But as the century ended, the threat of barbarian invasions on mainland Europe was growing. In 408 the legions were removed from Britain to meet this threat and in 410 the Emperor Honorius wrote to the cities of Britain to tell them that they must organize their own defence. The Pax Romana was at an end.

There were Anglo-Saxons living in England before the Romans left in 408, some of them brought from mainland Europe as mercenaries. Following the Roman departure they were joined by others, the eastern half of the country, from Hadrian's Wall to the Channel rapidly becoming 'Saxon'. In fact, as the 8th century chronicler Bede noted, there were three groups of settlers from Germany/Scandinavia. The north (including Yorkshire) and East Anglia were settled by Angles, while the Saxons held a belt now comprising Essex, Sussex, Middlesex and the counties that now occupy Wessex.

Kent, Hampshire and the Isle of Wight were occupied by the Jutes.

The Angles of Yorkshire founded two kingdoms, Deira which included the North York Moors, and Bernicia which lay to the north, a grouping that rapidly became a single kingdom, Northumbria, under the kingship of Edwin. Edwin was pagan, but married the Saxon princess Ethelburga, later converting to Christianity and being baptized in York's first minster on Easter Day 627. It is Edwin's minister Lilla who lies beneath Lilla Howe (visited by one of the walks described here – Walk 21), buried there after sacrificing himself to protect the King during an assassination attempt.

The Angles of Yorkshire left their mark on the country's place-names, the suffixes '-ley', '-ton' and '-ham' referring to their settlements. But many of the names frequently encountered – dale, beck, rigg, fell, gill, scar, moss and the suffixes '-by' and '-sett' on village names (the latter from *saetr*, a summer dwelling) – are Norse rather than Anglian. There had been Norse raids and invasions of Northumbria during the late 8th and early 9th centuries and there were probably already Norse settlements in remote valleys. Then, in 865, there was a full-scale Norse invasion. Caught unprepared – they were involved in a tribal feud – the Angles were driven south, the Norse raiders establishing their own kingdom. On 1 November 866 they took York, establishing the Norse city of Jorvik, a name that lives on in one of the city's finest museums/visitor centres.

Although King Alfred repulsed the Norse invaders at the border of Wessex, it was to be 150 years before the Anglo-Saxons recaptured Northumbria, fighting against formidable Norse leaders with unsettling names such as Eric Bloodaxe. So long did it take that there was hardly time for a celebration before the Normans had invaded southern England. Indeed, one of the reasons for the Saxon King Harold's defeat at Hastings may have been the forced march his men had made from a battle against the Norse King Harald (supported by Harold's brother Tostig, exiled by Harold in 1065 and seeking to take Wessex) at Stamford Bridge, near York, just nineteen days earlier. As the Normans moved north to secure their new realm they were met by increasingly belligerent opposition. That in Yorkshire was as strong as anywhere, the Norse settlers who remained, and the Saxon settlers who had followed the Saxons' northern march against the Norse, combining to resist William the Conqueror's army. A castle was built at York in 1068, manned by 500 men. It was attacked and taken, retaken and repaired and promptly attacked again. William himself came north to review the situation. His solution was as effective as it was ruthless, the 'harrying of the north' involving wholesale destruction of land and villages. One contemporary account notes that slaughtered bodies lay rotting in the fields because there was no one left to bury them. Norse invasions (and who could blame them for using the cover of civil disruption to try to regain their kingdom?) were repelled and resistance stamped out. New castles were built at York, Northallerton, Richmond and Pontefract, and Yorkshire fell silent.

In the peace that followed the Norman pacification of Yorkshire the great monastic houses were founded and the agriculture of the country was established, with sheep in the uplands and crops on the fertile lowlands. But Yorkshire's influence on English history had not yet ended. It is often said that the history of York is the history of England, and this was never more so than during the Wars of the Roses when the Lancastrian Red Rose and leaders called Henry fought the Yorkist White Rose and leaders called Edward or Richard. Only when Richard III was defeated by Henry Tudor (who become Henry VII) at Bosworth Field in 1485 did peace return. It lasted only fifty years, Henry VIII's Dissolution of the Monasteries leading to the Pilgrimage of Grace (chiefly centred on Yorkshire) in 1536. Robert Aske formed an army, took Pontefract Castle and marched on Hull and Doncaster. The rebellion was defeated and Aske was executed, but Yorkshire rose again thirty years later in support of the Catholic cause. That revolt, too, was put down, but it is worth remembering that Guy Fawkes was a Yorkshireman. The independence of thought – some might even say the Yorkshireman's enthusiasm for fighting authority – that has characterized the county ever since can be seen in those actions, and its origins can be seen in the battles against the Normans – William might have subdued southern England and been crowned (by Aldred, the Anglo-Danish Archbishop of York) at Westminster, but he was not king here. Not yet.

In 1639 Yorkshire rebuffed another king. Charles I had come to York to demand money from his loyal Yorkshiremen to mount a campaign against the Scots who were objecting to attempts to make them use the English prayer book. Yorkshire declined to pay. Charles returned to London and summoned the Long Parliament. It, too, declined to give him the cash. In the face of this defiance the King was compelled to raise an army. On 22 August 1642 he raised his standard at Nottingham: it promptly fell over, hardly an auspicious start. Ironically Yorkshire took the Royalist side and it was at Marston Moor, to the west of York, that the decisive battle of the first phase of the Civil War was fought. There, in 1644, the Royalist army was heavily defeated by a Parliamentarian army that included a deputy commander whose brilliance assured the victory. His name was Oliver Cromwell.

Sir Thomas Fairfax, himself a Yorkshireman, secured York and subdued the county and, at King Charles' trial, fifteen of the judges were from Yorkshire. In a further irony, it was Fairfax who travelled to Holland to talk to the king-to-be when the county grew tired of the Protectorate.

Yorkshire had one more central role to play in the history of Britain: the Industrial Revolution relied on the country's coal reserves which underpinned the development of steam power and the machinery of the Revolution. Edmund Cartwright's power loom was first used at Doncaster in 1787, the West

Riding (together with Lancashire) soon becoming the power-house of British industrialization. Before the arrival of steam power the local production had been concentrated in the owners' mills, but the cottages – even the villages – were now replaced by the back-to-back terraces that are part of the northern myth so popular in southern England. The industrial belt that crosses Yorkshire between Leeds and Sheffield supports the myth, but the areas visited by the walks in this book – the Dales, the Moors, the Wolds and southern Pennines – prove that in fact the myth has more to do with prejudice than with reality.

THE BEST WALKS

The Yorkshire Dales

The predominant rock of the Yorkshire Dales is the Great Scar Limestone, a carboniferous (water-soluble) limestone laid down below a shallow sea that covered western Yorkshire some 350 million years ago. Beneath the sea was a bed of Ordovician and Silurian slates that is still visible in Ribblesdale and at the mid-point of the Thornton Force waterfall near Ingleton. The sea was clear and rich in shelled sea creatures, the shells being the building blocks of the limestone. After the limestone had been raised and solidified, the area was again submerged, this time beneath a muddier sea that overlaid the limestone with a series of sandstones, limestones and shale known as the Yoredale Series (after the ancient name for the dale now known as Wensleydale). It is the existence of this layer of Yoredale rock (and an overtopping of Millstone Grit) which gives Pen-y-ghent its distinctive shape, the various rock types eroding at different rates. Earth movements following the creation of the Yoredale rocks began the process of creating the landscape we see today. The major movement created the Mid-Craven Fault along which the Great Scar Limestone was exposed. The most spectacular exposure is at Malham Cove, though cliffs ('scars') are a feature of many of the walks described here.

The Great Scar Limestone defines the Dales, in terms of their vegetation, though the area's geography is as much due to the last Ice Age as to the underlying geology. The ice sculpted the land, creating the dales themselves and exposing sections of rock that were then eroded into the features we see today. Kilnsey Crag is a product of ice and weathering, and the fantastic limestone pavement above Malham Cove (the best of several in the area) was fashioned by erosion processes after the ice had chamfered the rock sheet smooth. Only when rainwater began to dissolve the limestone was the familiar 'clints' and 'grykes' pattern etched on to the pavement.

The same process of dissolution led to the creation of the caves and potholes that are such a feature of the area – and the walks described here. Cave formation also gave rise to Gordale Scar, one of the area's most dramatic features, and to the disappearance of healthy streams, with the creation of the dry valleys that troubled geologists until the process of limestone dissolution was better understood.

The earth movements responsible for the Mid-Craven Fault also allowed ore-bearing rock to intrude into the smooth evolutionary process of rock formation in the Dales. Although it was never a widespread occupation, for the ore-bearing intrusions were too localized, lead mining was important in the Dales, the Romans having mines as early as the 1st century AD. Production peaked in the late 18th and 19th centuries, but declined sharply at the end of the last century. There were mines at Greenhow Hill, near Nidderdale, but the main area was in Swaledale where the ruins of former mines and of the 'hushing' process of ore extraction still scar the landscape. Close by, on Tan Hill, coal was extracted, but the seams were thin and the coal of poor quality, and the mines were barely profitable. One of the walks described here (Walk 12) explores this old mining site, the scarring being compensated by a visit to England's highest inn. For the remainder of the Dales folk the chief occupation was, and is, sheep rearing, the ease with which water disappears and the thin, poor limestone soil making the area unsuitable for arable farming. The harsh climate and poor grass are also a trial for sheep, but hardy breeds have been evolved to tolerate these conditions. The main breed is the Swaledale, the second being the Dalesbred, a Swaledale/Scottish Blackface cross. The sheep, and the dry-stone walls that enclose them (walls that date from the early

19th century Enclosures Act, despite having the look of per-
manence that implies they are as old as the hills themselves),
are features that the Dales-walker grows to love. Indeed, it is
no surprise to discover that the emblem of the Yorkshire Dales
National Park is a Swaledale ram – a Swaledale tup, to use the
correct local term.

The National Park that embraces the Dales was designated
in 1954, the seventh of the National Parks of England and
Wales to be created. It covers an area of 680 square miles,
smaller in size only than the Lake District and Snowdonia
Parks. Scenically magnificent and geologically fascinating, the
Park is one of two main focuses of walking in this book.

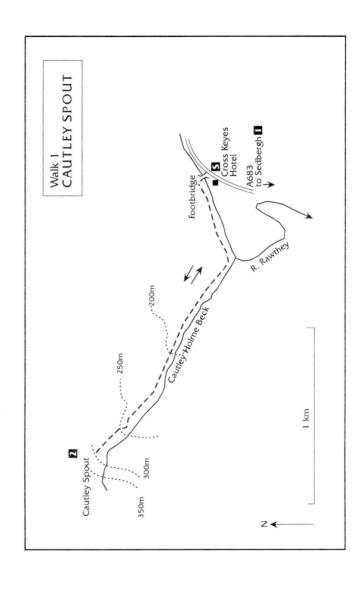

Walk 1
CAUTLEY SPOUT

Cross Keyes
Hotel

A683
to Sedbergh

Footbridge

R. Rawthey

Cautley·Holme Beck

-200m

250m

Cautley Spout

300m

350m

1 km

N

Walk 1 Cautley Spout

The focal point for this short walk at the extreme north-western corner of the National Park is Cautley Spout, a spectacular falls not only because of its length, but also because of its position in a magnificent wide valley.

Walk category: Easy (1.75 hours)

Length: 5 km (3 miles)

Ascent: 150 m (500 ft)

Maps: Landranger Sheet 98, Pathfinder Sheet 617

Starting and finishing point: At 698969, a layby on the north side of the A683 close to the Cross Keys Temperance Hotel. The hotel is situated about 8 km (5 miles) north-east of Sedbergh (see (1) Sedbergh) on the left side of the road to Kirby Stephen.

There is a footbridge below the layby: descend to this, cross and turn left along a clear path beside the River Rawthey. Eventually the path bears right, away from the river, following Cautley Holme Beck (an infeed of the Rawthey) towards Cautley Spout which is seen in the valley ahead.

   The path reaches the base of the fall (see (2) Cautley Spout) easily, but a scramble up a steep and occasionally unstable path is needed to reach the best viewpoints. Please take care, especially if you have children with you: although the path is clear enough the detours to the viewpoints can be slippery and the drop to the falls is long and uninviting.

To return to the start, reverse the outward route, admiring the views to Baugh Fell ahead.

(1) Sedbergh

This busy little market town has several odd claims to fame. One is that, although it is the largest town in the Yorkshire Dales National Park, it is actually in Cumbria! Another relates to the famous boys' school founded here in 1525 by Roger Lupton, a canon of Windsor and provost of Eton. Lupton's foundation was for 'theym of Sedber' though it has today widened its catchment area, being one of Britain's foremost public schools. William Wordsworth's son is numbered among its old boys (as is Will Carling) though the son of another Lakeland poet, Samuel Taylor Coleridge, was sacked from his position as a master at the school after a particularly memorable drinking session. One early, and very successful, headmaster was called Posthumous Wharton: presumably his parents believed that after lasting him a lifetime the name would be good for eternity. A further claim is that George Fox, the founder of the Quaker movement, preached under the yew tree in St Andrew's Church. There is a Quaker Meeting house in Brigflatts, a hamlet to the south-west of the town. Finally, Bonnie Prince Charlie is said to have hidden in the chimney of Webster's Chemists, a fine early 17th century house.

(2) Cautley Spout

The Spout is a waterfall over 200 m (nearly 700 ft) in length, though this is not a single drop, but a series of fine falls down the mountainside. The Spout is set in wonderful, rugged country, with the Howgill Fells to the west, and Baugh Fell and Mallerstang to the east. Geologically the rounded Howgill Fells are part of the Lake District rather than the Yorkshire Dales, the sandstones and slates that form them being much

Cautley Spout

older than the rock below the Dales. They also differ in being common land and so have no walls, a distinct difference from the upland areas to the east. On Mallerstang is the evocatively named Wild Boar Fell, where Sir Richard Musgrave is said to have killed the last wild boar in England in the 15th century.

Walk 2 Richmond

In addition to its National Parks, the Wolds and Pennines, a plethora of picturesque villages and a fascinating section of coast, Yorkshire also has a number of fine towns. This short walk uses an old railway track from which there are excellent views of Richmond, delightfully set on the River Swale, before exploring the historic town centre.

Walk category: Easy (1.5 hours)

Length: 5.5 km (3.5 miles)

Ascent: 20 m (65 ft)

Maps: Landranger Sheet 92, Pathfinder Sheet 609

Starting and finishing point: At 174011, in the Market Place, Richmond.There is adequate parking in the Market Place, but Richmond operates a disc parking system and newcomers to the town must obtain a (free) disc from local shops.

Go to the bottom end of the Market Place (see (1) Richmond) and turn right along Millgate, following it downhill towards the River Swale. Turn left along Park Wynd, soon bearing right on a path that goes under an arch. The path goes below Richmond School to reach a fork near a millstone. Bear right to descend to Station (or Mercury) Bridge over the River Swale. Soon after going beneath the bridge the path turns left away from the river. Continue along it to reach a house, on the right, at a road end.

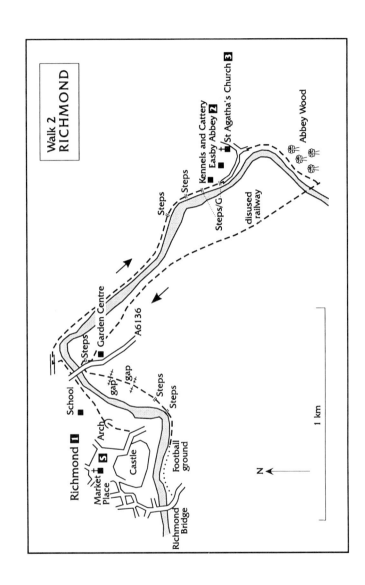

Walk 2
RICHMOND

Richmond **1**

Market Place **S**

School

Castle

Arch

Football ground

Richmond Bridge

gap

gap

Steps

Steps

Steps

Garden Centre

A6136

Steps

Steps

Steps/G

Kennels and Cattery

Easby Abbey **2**

St Agatha's Church **3**

disused railway

Abbey Wood

N

1 km

Turn right along the track which is a continuation of the road. When the track forks, bear right to return to the river, following the bank to reach steps up to a stile. Cross and continue to another stile at the Abbey Mill Kennels and Cattery. A stile beyond the Kennels gives access to a drive past the ruins of Easby Abbey (see (2) Easby Abbey). The walk continues parallel to the river, but it is worth the short detour to the left to visit St Agatha's Church (see (3) St Agatha's Church).

Continue along the riverbank, going through more woodland (Abbey Wood) to reach a fork. Take the gravel track which rises very slightly to reach an old railway bridge over the River Swale. Turn sharp right over the bridge and follow the old trackbed back towards Richmond. There are fine views of the town from here.

As the old track approaches Station Bridge, go through the bollards ahead to reach a garden centre, on the left, at the site of the old station. Now walk towards the bridge, but do not cross. Instead, go right, down steps, and turn back under the bridge on a path that bears left, away from the river, to reach a fence gap. Go through this and another gap through the fence ahead, then continue to reach a stile. Cross this to reach a path that soon follows the river. Go over another stile, then follow the path to its end. Bear left through a wall gap and turn right along the edge of the Richmond Town Football Ground. Walk past the changing rooms and out to a road. Turn right and follow the road over Richmond Bridge, pausing to admire the view of the castle. Now continue straight up Bridge Street, turning first right into New Road to return to the Market Place.

(1) Richmond

An early visitor to Richmond noted that the 'towne standeth on unequal grounde', a succinct description of the town's site beside the River Swale. The castle, built in 1071 by Alain Rufus to defend this important frontier site – at that time Norman

England did not extend much further north – is one of the most dramatically positioned in the country. It is also interesting for its architecture. The keep, a 30 m (100 ft) tower, stands, unusually, at the gate, and Scollard's Hall, built in 1080, is one of the earliest domestic castle buildings in Britain. The view of the town from the top of the keep is memorable. Inside the castle, visitors can see the detention cells used during the First World War for imprisoning conscientious objectors who had been conscripted into non-combatant units but who declined to obey orders. In 1916 some of these men were shipped to France and court martialled. They were sentenced to death, but the sentences were all commuted to imprisonment with hard labour. Also inside the castle, beside the evocative ruins of the old towers and walls, visitors can see a plaque commemorating the time spent here by General Baden-Powell, the founder of the Boy Scout movement. Baden-Powell commanded the Northumbrian Division of the Territorial Army from 1908 to 1910 during which time it had its headquarters at the castle. The castle is in the hands of English Heritage and can be visited during standard opening hours.

Richmond castle is said to be the resting place of King Arthur and his knights, sleeping silently as they await the call to rescue England. A more recent legend relates an incident in the 18th century when, it is claimed, soldiers at the castle found the entrance to a tunnel beneath the keep. There had long been rumours of an underground link between the castle and Easby Abbey and so the soldiers decided to investigate. A drummer boy was therefore sent into the tunnel and as he walked towards the abbey the soldiers above ground followed the noise of his drumming which could be clearly heard. About half-way to the abbey the drumming suddenly stopped. The drummer boy was never seen again. Today a stone close to the walk suggested here commemorates the tale. Legend also has

Richmond Castle and the River Swale

it that the ghost of a drummer boy can sometimes be heard beating a tattoo as he patrols the tunnel.

The Market Place, where the walk starts, is huge – it is the largest horseshoe-shaped market place in Britain and has much of interest. The obelisk marks the spot where the original market cross stood. Close by is Trinity Church, now the museum of the Green Howards Regiment where modern display techniques bring the history of the regiment alive. Two other museums in the town are also worth visiting. The Georgian Theatre Museum is attached to the theatre, one of the most complete of its age in the country. The museum has a unique collection of period scenery as well as other fascinating theatrical items. The Richmondshire Museum, a short step away from the Market Place in Ryders Wynd, has an equally fascinating collection of items illustrating life in the local area in bygone times. The collection includes a James Herriot Surgery Set named for the famous veterinarian who lived locally. Elsewhere, visitors can see Hill House in Darlington Road where Frances L'Anson, the original 'Lass of Richmond Hill' lived. The words of the song were written by Lawrence McNally, a lawyer and poet, who was captivated by her beauty and married her in 1787.

(2) Easby Abbey

The abbey was constructed in 1155 for Premonstratensian canons and enjoyed a quiet, undistinguished history punctuated by occasional visits from Scottish raiding parties. It was dissolved in 1536. The ruins include remnants of many of the abbey's domestic buildings, together with the abbey church. Premonstratensian canons were allowed to serve as priests, the abbey church acting as the parish church of Easby, a fact that ensured its survival. The ruins are in the care of English Heritage and can be visited during standard opening hours.

(3) St Agatha's Church

The church, named for a 3rd century Sicilian martyr, dates largely from the 12th century and has a fine font from that time. The cross shaft in the chancel is not the original, which has been taken to the Victoria and Albert Museum in London.

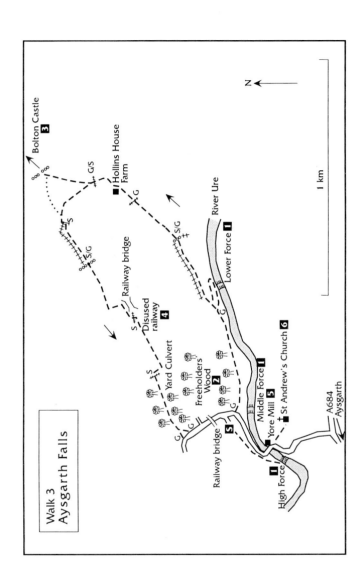

Walk 3
Aysgarth Falls

Bolton Castle **3**

Hollins House Farm

G/S

G

S/G

River Ure

Lower Force **1**

Railway bridge

Disused railway **4**

Yard Culvert

S

Freeholders' Wood **2**

G

G

Railway bridge

3

Middle Force **1**

Yore Mill **5**

St Andrew's Church **6**

High Force **1**

A684 Aysgarth

N

1 km

Walk 3 Aysgarth Falls

This short walk visits the most popular waterfalls in the National Park and, after Malham Cove, the most popular scenic spot too. There are actually three falls at Aysgarth, the Middle and Lower Falls are visited on the walk, the Upper Falls requiring a very short extension.

Walk category: Easy/Intermediate (2 hours)

Length: 6.5 km (4 miles)

Ascent: 50 m (165 ft)

Maps: Landranger Sheet 98, Outdoor Leisure Sheet 30

Starting and finishing point: At 012887, the car-park at the National Park Centre near Aysgarth. The car-park lies to the east of Aysgarth village. If you are approaching from the Hardraw side, go through the village and turn left on the road to Caperby to reach Yore Mill and its museum. If approaching from Northallerton, turn right for the mill before the village is reached. Go past the Mill, cross the River Ure – with the Upper Falls on your left – and turn left soon after to reach the National Park Centre.

From the car-park, follow the signed path beside the entrance road and turn right along the road back to the mill. Soon, go left along a path signed for Middle Force and Lower Force. The first falls, Middle Force (see (1) Aysgarth Falls) can be viewed from a platform reached by steps descending to the right of the path. Now continue along the path through beautiful woodland to reach a gate on the right. The woodland is Freeholders' Wood (see (2) Freeholders' Wood).

Do not go through the gate: instead continue along the path, soon reaching a path fork. Bear right and follow the path to view the Lower Force (see (1) Aysgarth Falls). Continue along the path past the falls, climbing up to reach the gate passed earlier in the walk. Go through and turn right to return to the path fork.

Now bear left along the other branch (signed for Castle Bolton), following it to a fence and walking with the fence on your left to reach a stile/gate. Cross the stile and climb the field beyond to reach a gate into Hollins House Farm. Bear left through the farm and then right beyond the last building to go along a metalled lane. Go through a gate and continue along the metalled lane for a few metres. The official right of way now goes right along a signed field path, heading towards a stile over a wall. Go that way for a good view of Castle Bolton (see (3) Bolton Castle). When you reach the wall, bear left away from it, following a raised bank across the field to return to the metalled lane. It is easier to just walk along the lane and that is what most walkers do, but the right of way (and the view of the castle) requires this detour.

Cross the lane and go over a stile on the right, walking through the undergrowth to reach a fence. Turn left and follow the fence – the undergrowth can be tiresome here if there have been few walkers on the path – to a stile/gate. Go over and cross the field beyond heading for a lone sycamore and then a hawthorn to reach a track. Bear left along the track to reach a tunnel under the trackbed of an old railway (see (4) Leyburn to Hawes Railway). The section of overgrown footpath just beyond the metalled lane was also along the old track.

Bear right to reach a stile, cross and climb up on to the old trackbed, turning right along it. The exit from the track is not signed, but easy to find: leave the track as soon as a hedge appears at right angles – if you go as far as a crossing fence with an absent bridge and a yard beyond, you have gone too far, but only by a few metres. Descend and follow the hedge (with it on your left) for a few metres to reach a squeeze stile. Go over and follow the path beyond to a path fork. Bear right and walk through fine woodland to reach another fork. Either branch will do here as they both reach the same road within a few metres. Turn left along the road, soon passing a road, left, to the yard glimpsed earlier. Go under the old railway bridge, pausing to admire the craftsmanship of the brickwork, and turn right to return to the car-park.

To extend the walk to High Force, the Upper Falls, go to the rear of the car-park and follow a path which descends to the left to reach the road at the bridge over the Ure. The building across the river, and the other side of the road, is Yore Mill (see (5) Yore Mill). From the mill steps lead up to Aysgarth Church (see (6) Aysgarth Church). The walk does not go on to the road, going though a gate and continuing beside the river to reach a gate and honesty box just before the Upper Falls. Reverse the route to return to the car-park.

(1) Aysgarth Falls

Aysgarth's name derives from the old word for the oak, the local woods being one of the last remnants of ancient Dales woodland. As at Hardraw, the three Aysgarth waterfalls are caused by the erosion of layers of soft shale that lie between layers of hard limestone of the Yoredale Series rock. The layers of soft and hard rock lie almost horizontally, erosion of the soft shale leaving overhanging lips of harder limestone. When the lips become unstable they break off as blocks, but leave behind pavements of flat rock, the falls being a series of jumps over these pavements. Only at the Lower Force has a significant fall been created. Each of the falls, or forces, is a delight, framed by beautiful woodland that is alive with flowers in spring and set off by steep limestone cliffs. The delights of the falls were

noticed by the artist Turner long before they became generally popular, his painting of Aysgarth helping to establish the falls as part of the round of the well-bred tourist.

(2) Freeholders' Wood

The freeholders of the name were local residents of Caperby who had (and retain) the right to gather firewood. The wood's trees (chiefly its hazels) were cut close to the ground resulting in a series of new shoots being generated. These were allowed to grow and were then cut for firewood, the process yielding both more wood than could be gathered by conventional felling and a continuous supply. The wood is now owned by the National Park, but its hazel stands are being coppiced for the benefit of the freeholders. Freeholder's rights are limited to thirty-one properties – not individuals – in Caperby and include not only the right to gather firewood (known as estovers) but also the right to fish in the River Ure, a right known as piscary.

   Although hazel dominates the wood there are also several other deciduous species, the mix making a perfect habitat for animals, including roe deer, and birds. In spring the woodland floor is carpeted with primroses and wood anemones and, after they have flowered, with bluebells.

(3) Bolton Castle

The castle was built in the late 14th century by Richard, Lord Scrope, one-time Chancellor to Richard II, on the site of his own manor house. As a consequence, the design was part-fortification, part-home, as the large living-rooms, each with its own fireplace, suggest. The castle was one of the first to have proper chimneys from the fireplaces. In July 1568 the castle became the prison of Mary, Queen of Scots who was kept here for six months before being transferred to Tutbury Castle in

Lower Force, Aysgarth

Staffordshire. Given that the Queen was accompanied by six ladies-in-waiting and a retinue of fifty servants it is a moot point whether prison is the correct word, though, of course, she was not at liberty to leave and her confinement (here and elsewhere) did end in her execution.

During the Civil War the castle was held by Royalists who resisted a Parliamentarian siege for over twelve months before surrendering. Perhaps as retribution, Bolton was partially demolished after the war, though it was later restored. One of the four corner towers remained unstable, however, and collapsed in 1761 during a violent storm. Following further restoration Bolton has now been opened to the public. It is well worth visiting, being arguably the finest castle of its type in Britain.

(4) Leyburn to Hawes Railway

Walkers who have completed the Hardraw Force walk (Walk 5) have already seen the terminus station of the North Eastern Railway Company's line from Leyburn to Hawes. The line opened in 1878 and carried both freight – quarried flagstones, milk, butter and cheese out of Wensleydale and all the requirements of life back in – and passengers. The line closed to passenger traffic in 1954 and to freight in 1964, though the line still operates from Redmire to Leyburn, carrying stone from the Redmire quarry. The now trackless line is private property, apart from a small section near Aysgarth. The café and toilets at the National Park Centre at the start of the walk are housed in old railway workers' cottages.

Very recently, part of the old line has been reopened by the Ministry of Defence; the Wensleydale Railway Association is attempting to reopen the whole line for the benefit of both locals and visitors. It is hoped that the entire link from Garsdale to the Settle–Carlisle line will be opened by the year 2000, and the purchase of lines for the new track is already going ahead.

(5) Yore Mill

The mill, a 19th century building occupying the site of an earlier mill which was destroyed by fire, was used for both cloth making and corn milling at various times and is most famous for having produced the red shirts worn by Garibaldi's troops when they invaded Sicily in 1861 as part of the Risorgimento, the movement to re-establish the kingdom of Italy. Today the mill houses the G. W. Shaw Carriage Collection under the name of the Carriage Museum of Horse-drawn Vehicles. There is also a craft shop and a tearoom.

(6) Aysgarth Church

St Andrew's Church, once the mother church of upper Wensleydale, was rebuilt in 1866. Until 11 July 1996 the church housed a 1000-year-old Northumbrian cross-head found, in 1968, by the vicar's young son as he was playing in the churchyard. Sadly on that day in 1996 the crosshead was stolen and has not (at the time of writing) been recovered. The church's other great treasure remains. This is the rood screen on the east side of the chancel. This magnificent painted and gilded carved wood screen was brought to the church after the dissolution of Jervaulx Abbey. The vicar's stall close to the screen also came from Jervaulx where it was the abbot's stall. The abbot's emblem of crozier and mitre can still be seen on one end.

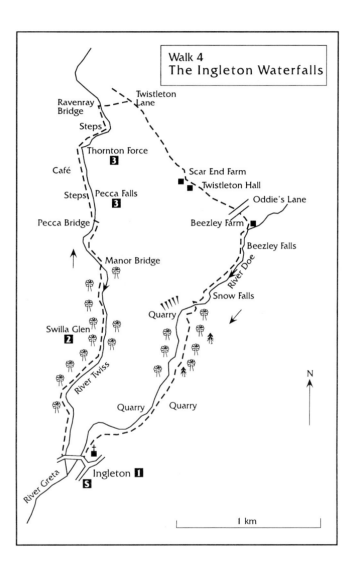

Walk 4
The Ingleton Waterfalls

Twistleton Lane

Ravenray Bridge

Steps

Thornton Force 3

Café

Steps   Pecca Falls 3

Pecca Bridge

Scar End Farm
Twistleton Hall

Oddie's Lane

Beezley Farm

Beezley Falls

Manor Bridge

River Doe

Snow Falls

Quarry

Swilla Glen 2

River Twiss

Quarry   Quarry

N

Ingleton 1

River Greta

S

1 km

Walk 4 The Ingleton Waterfalls

The masses of Ingleborough, Whernside and Gragareth define the dales in which the Rivers Doe and Twiss flow. As they near Ingleton each of these rivers flows through tight gorges in which their waters make spectacular waterfalls.

Ingleton has been a tourist centre since the railway arrived in 1849, but it was not until 1884 when a group of locals formed the Ingleton Improvement Society and started to improve the paths around the village with paving, bridges and steps that it really took off. The path followed by the walk described here opened in 1885: in 1888 over 4000 people paid 1d (one old penny) to follow the route. It is one of the most impressive lowland walks in the Dales, visiting several fine falls and linking the valleys of the Doe and Twiss.

Walk category: Easy (2.5 hours)

Length: 7 km (4.5 miles)

Ascent: 180 m (590 ft)

Maps: Landranger Sheet 98, Outdoor Leisure Sheet 2

Starting and finishing point: The car-park at the Tourist Information Centre in Ingleton. The car-park is well signed.

From the car-park, go down the steps on the right side of the Information Centre and turn right. Bear left down The Raike (opposite the Three Horseshoes Inn) and turn left at the bottom. The parish church is to the right here (see (1) Ingleton). Cross the bridges over the Rivers Twiss and Doe and then turn right to reach the car-park and start of the Waterfalls Walk, paying the small entrance fee. The route beyond is virtually paved throughout, making map, compass and even a route description redundant. A few notes are given here in order to locate the points of interest along the way.

The starting wide track narrows when it reaches the bank of the River Twiss. Go through a kissing gate to reach the lovely wooded gorge of Swilla Glen, the first highlight of the walk (see (2) Swilla Glen). The route goes up and down steepish steps within the gorge.

When the path reaches a footbridge (Manor Bridge) cross and continue along the opposite riverbank to reach another footbridge (Pecca Bridge). Recross the river here and climb steep steps to reach the first waterfall (actually a series of falls). This is Pecca Falls (see (3) Waterfalls). The path stays very close to the falls as it climbs to the top of the gorge and a handy refreshment area. The path now continues easily to reach the second waterfall, Thornton Force (see (3) Waterfalls).

Continue up steps beside Thornton Falls to reach another footbridge (Ravenray Bridge). Cross and go up steps to reach a gate. Go through and turn right along a walled lane (Twistleton Lane). From the lane there are fine views towards Ingleton and the scar end of the long Whernside ridge.

Follow the lane to Twistleton Hall, on the right, going over a stile there and continuing to reach another soon after. Ahead now is the elegant, imposing mass of Ingleborough. Follow the path to a lane (Oddie's Lane), crossing it and following the metalled track ahead for a few metres before turning right, in front of a farmhouse (Beezley Farm, another refreshment stop), to go along a track. Bear left with this track, going through a gate and continuing to reach a signed footpath on the left. Follow this path downhill into the wooded gorge of the Rive Doe. The path now follows the river, soon reaching the Doe's first waterfall, Beezley Falls.

Continue along the riverbank, the path going through ever more dramatic scenery as it follows the top of the river gorge. At one point there is an observation bridge where the delights of the tight, wooded gorge and the river's combination of cascades and deep pools can be savoured at close quarters. Beyond this bridge Snow Falls is passed: continue to reach a footbridge. Cross and follow the opposite riverbank, soon passing several old quarries. Skirwith Quarry, from which gritstone for road building is still extracted, can be seen to the east.

Go over a footbridge across a feeder stream of the River Doe, exiting from the woodland to see Ingleton just a short distance ahead. When the path reaches a lane, bear left, reversing the first few metres of the walk to regain the start.

(1) Ingleton

Although in the past Ingleton has depended on coal mining, cotton mills, lime kilns and stone quarries for its livelihood, its main industry is now tourism, the village being a centre for walkers heading towards Ingleborough and Whernside, cavers aiming for Ingleborough and those wishing to see the waterfalls visited on this walk.

The village church, dedicated to St Mary the Virgin, is a delight, long and low with a sturdy tower. Inside there is a fine Norman font which was discovered in 1830 in the River Greta. It is assumed that it was hidden during the Civil War when it was feared the Puritans would have smashed it. The church also has a 'Vinegar' Bible. These are so called because due to a printer's error a 1717 printing of the Bible had the heading 'Parable of the Vinegar' instead of 'Parable of the Vineyard' above Luke 20.

The viaduct over the River Greta – as the combined Rivers Twiss and Doe is known – carried the long since defunct railway. The starting car-park for the walk is on the site of the old station.

(2) Swilla Glen

The glen is a marvellous example of a tight limestone gorge, its walls covered with mosses, liverworts and ferns. Some of the mosses and liverworts are rare, but it is the ferns which catch the eye. Look out for hart's tongue, maidenhair spleenwort, male fern and common polypody as well as the rarer brittle bladder fern. The surrounding woodland is mixed deciduous, with oak, birch and ash dominating.

(3) Waterfalls

Geologically the walk from Ingleton to Thornton Force is extremely interesting as it crosses two major faults – the South and North Craven Faults – and a minor fault close to the North Craven Fault. As a result the underlying rock changes from the normal carboniferous limestone of the Dales to a mix of Ordovician shales, slates and sandstones and then back to limestone again.

Pecca Falls, which is not a true waterfall but a series of cascades – though it is no less attractive for that – lies on the Ordovician rock, the series of cascades being created by differential erosion between the softer slate layers and the harder sandstone layers. Thornton Force is a conventional waterfall, the Twiss leaping from a tight gorge into more open country that allows a real appreciation of the beauty of the falls. Geologically the fall is extremely interesting. The upper section is over a band of grey limestone bedded horizontally, while the lower section is over vertically bedded green Ingleton slate. Between these two rock bands is a layer of conglomerate – pebbles held together by a sandy 'cement'. These pebbles really are from a beach, their roundness and smoothness created by the wash of a sea about 400 million years ago, the shallow seabeneath which the upper limestone was laid down. It is possible to go behind the falls at about

Pecca Falls

half-height, but care is needed as a slip could be result in serious injury.

Though smaller, Beezley and the aptly named Snow Falls on the River Doe are also very picturesque.

Walk 5 Hardraw Force

A visit to the longest single drop falls in Yorkshire (and England). The walk is interesting in that a small section actually lies through an inn! A fee is payable but few begrudge the toll for one of Yorkshire's finest sights.

Walk category: Easy (2 hours)

Length: 8 km (5 miles)

Ascent: 120 m (394 ft)

Maps: Landranger Sheet 98, Outdoor Leisure Sheet 30

Starting and finishing point: At 876899, the car-park by the National Park Centre and Dales Countryside Museum, Hawes.

From the car-park at Hawes (see (1) Hawes), go out on to the road through the last part of the village and turn right along the road to Muker. After about 100 m, turn left, as signed for the Pennine Way, and follow a paved path across a field to rejoin the road. Turn left and follow the road over Haylands Bridge, which crosses the River Ure. Beyond the bridge the road hugs the river for a few metres, then bears away. Soon after there is a signed footpath for Hardraw on the left. Do not take this: instead, continue for another 100 m or so and then turn left up steps, signed for the Pennine Way, to reach a gate.

  Go through the gate and follow the Pennine Way along a clear path, much of it paved, across several fields linked by stiles or gates. The Way eventually emerges on the road in Hardraw, opposite the church and the Green Dragon Inn. The

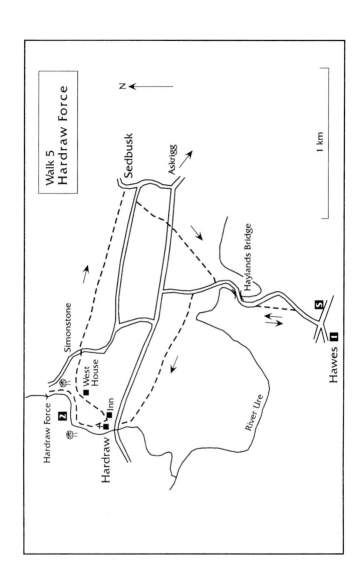

Walk 5
Hardraw Force

N

1 km

Sedbusk

Askrigg

Simonstone

West House

Hardraw Force

Hardraw

Inn

Haylands Bridge

River Ure

Hawes

S

1

2

first building on the inn site was a grange of Fountains Abbey, giving the inn a history of welcoming guests that goes back over 700 years. To visit Hardraw Force, which is on private land, it is now necessary to go through the Green Dragon, although stopping for refreshment *en route* (or on the return) is perfectly acceptable!

Go into the inn, pay the entrance fee, go out of the back door and follow the path past the church and beside the river. After viewing the falls (see (2) Hardraw Force) return to the inn and the road in Hardraw. Turn left and immediately left again beside the inn. Follow the wall on the left to reach a stile, go over and walk uphill along a path to reach a house on the right (West House). Go through a gate and bear right to reach a stile. Cross to reach the Simonstone Hall Hotel and turn right along the drive to reach a road. Turn left, soon reaching a signed stile on the right. Follow the track beyond through a gate to reach the farm buildings and continue over a ladder stile. The path now heads eastwards in a straight line crossing a great number of fields linked by stiles or gates towards the village of Sedbusk seen ahead. When you emerge in the village (Shutt Lane), turn right and walk to a road (Sedbusk Lane).

Turn right for a few metres, then go left over a stile and follow a path signed for Haylands Bridge. The path goes downhill to reach the Hardraw–Askrigg road. Cross the road, go through a signed gate and continue along a path, going through another gate and over a fine old packhorse bridge before reaching the road close to Haylands Bridge. Turn left and reverse the outward route back to the starting car-park.

(1) Hawes

Hawes – known to the locals as T'Haas – is the market town for Wensleydale, one of the few Yorkshire Dales not named for its river. The river in Wensleydale is the Ure, Wensley being one of the dale's villages. Hawes is an ancient site, probably named by Yorkshire's Norse settlers for its position at the *hals*,

the neck or narrowest point of the valley. The present church dates from the 19th century, but there is a record of Richard II appointing a priest to the village in 1483. The National Park Centre and car-park mark the station of the Midland Railway Company's branch line from Garsdale and the North Eastern Railway Company's line from Leyburn, an unusual joint usage. The centre is the old station building, the Dales Countryside Museum occupying an old goods warehouse. The station master lived in the house to the left of the car-park entrance. The railway was chiefly freight, the main outgoing freight being sandstone flagstones quarried from the Yoredale Series of rocks. The flagstones were used as roofing slates. The main quarries were close to the villages of Hardraw and Simonstone. Though the stone quarries and railway are now closed, Wensleydale cheese is still made in Hawes.

Depending upon your point of view, Hawes is worth visiting or avoiding on Tuesdays – market day – when stalls line the main street and many hundreds of sheep fill the pens in Leyburn Road. It is estimated that over 100,000 sheep pass through the Hawes market each year.

The town is also the centre for the production of Wensleydale cheese, at the Wensleydale Creamery. A few years ago the Creamery was threatened with closure, but the outcry which followed the realization that all Wensleydale cheese production would then have been in Lancashire caused a successful rescue. Today visitors can visit the Creamery's Cheese Experience Centre where cheese making is explained (and can be seen from a viewing gallery) and white, blue and smoked cheese can be bought.

Another fine museum is housed in the old railway station, in the same building that houses the National Park Centre. The Dales Countryside Museum explores the history of the valley from the last Ice Age to the present and has a fascinating

The stream below Hardraw Force

collection of old tools and craft objects. Close to the museum is one of the few handmade ropeworks left in Britain. Here, visitors can watch the process of rope-making.

Those interested in exploring Hawes at greater length – and it is well worth the time – should buy a copy of the Hawes Town Trail, available from the local newsagent in the main street.

(2) Hardraw Force

The waterfall was created by a feeder stream of the River Ure cutting into the soft shale beside a hard outcrop of Yoredale Series sandstone/limestone, a much harder rock. The banded nature of the rock is obvious behind the falls, the lighter Yoredale rock bands lying above the darker shale bands. Over this banded rock the stream free-falls for almost 30 metres (100 ft) into a pool known as The Dub. This fall makes Hardraw the longest single drop fall in England, though it should be noted that the distinction has to be made between above ground and below ground falls: there are several waterfalls in cave systems which have longer single drops than Hardraw. The volume of water dropping over the falls is quite small, so the force is at its best after heavy or continuous rain. As it is also possible to walk behind the falls – be careful, the rocks are smooth and slippery – dry weather has its compensations, the spray being less drenching.

As the walker leaves the Green Dragon Inn, the remnants of a bandstand can be seen (on the left, just after the footbridge). From 1885 the gorge was the venue for a popular brass-band competition, the walker still being able to see the tiered seats cut into the hillside opposite the bandstand for spectators. The competition lasted until about 1900, was revived in the 1920s and has recently been revived again.

Hardraw saw another event, but this time only a one-off, when the famous tightrope artist Blondin crossed the falls. This remarkable feat was made even more so by the fact that Blondin stopped in the middle of the rope to cook an omelette.

To the north of the falls Shaw Gill Wood is a beautiful place with two smaller, but very attractive, falls.

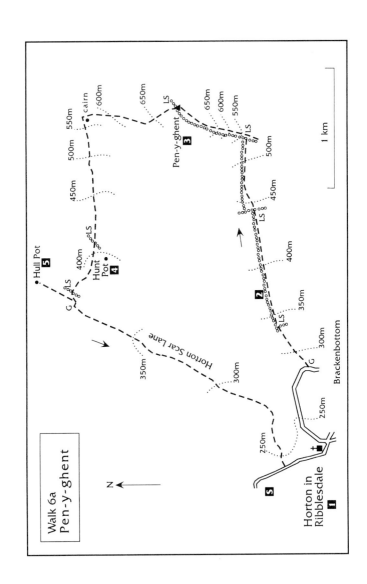

Walk 6a
Pen-y-ghent

N

Horton in
Ribblesdale

Brackenbottom

Horton Scar Lane

Hull Pot

Hunt
Pot

Pen-y-ghent

cairn

1 km

250m
250m
300m
350m
400m
450m
500m
550m
600m
650m

Walk 6 The Three Peaks

The Three Peaks of Whernside (the highest in Yorkshire), Ingleborough and Pen-y-ghent are obvious targets for the walker, either singly or as one of England's finest challenge walks. Here we ascend each in turn.

Walk 6a Pen-y-ghent

Although a reasonably straightforward route, the final ascent to the summit is steep and involves a little climbing.

Walk category: Intermediate/Difficult (3 hours)

Length: 10.5 km (6.5 miles)

Ascent: 500 m (1640 ft)

Maps: Landranger Sheet 98, Outdoor Leisure Sheet 2

Starting and finishing point: At 808726, the car-park in Horton in Ribblesdale.

From the car-park, turn right along the main road (the B6479) through the village (see (1) Horton in Ribblesdale) passing the church on your left. Cross Horton Bridge over a feeder stream of the River Ribble and turn left immediately, along the lane to Brackenbottom. Just as you approach the first building of this pleasant hamlet (a barn on the left), there is a signed footpath also on the left: take this, following a wall on your left, and climbing towards the southern edge of Pen-y-ghent.

Go over a ladder stile and continue, still with a wall on your left (see (2) Drystone Walling) and with the opening panorama of Fountains Fell, named for Fountains Abbey which owned the land in medieval times, to the right. Go over another ladder stile and follow a stepped path up to reach another. Go over this and turn left for the final steep climb. The climb stays to the right of the peak's craggy western edge, but does involve some scrambling.

From the trig. point summit (see (3) Pen-y-ghent) go over the ladder stile and head downhill along a rocky path that soon reaches the edge of the western cliff-line. Bear right along the top of the cliffs to reach a prominent cairn and a footpath sign. Turn sharp left here, following the signed direction for Horton. The path descends across moorland to reach a ladder stile over a wall. Cross this to reach Hunt Pot, to the left (see (4) Hunt Pot). Continue along the path to reach another ladder stile. Cross this to reach a t-junction of paths. Turn right here for a short detour to Hull Pot (see (5) Hull Pot).

Return to the path junction, turning right now and going through a gate into Horton Scar Lane. Follow this walled lane all the way back to Horton, turning right when the main village road is reached to return to the starting car-park.

(1) Horton in Ribblesdale

Horton is a somewhat scattered village, memorable chiefly for its welcoming inns and café, and for a delightful little church. The south door of St Oswald's Church is Norman, as is the font, but the solid tower is later, dating from the 16th century. In the west window there is a fragment of stained glass from Jervaulx, rescued when the abbey there was dissolved. A village tradition maintains that the lead for the roof was mined near Hull Pot by Horton's menfolk, while the lych-gate is roofed with massive Horton slate.

Pen-y-ghent from the south-west

The village houses are an object lesson in the development of some Dales villages. At the eastern village edge there are 17th century yeoman farmer houses while the Victorian terraces were built when the railway arrived. Nearer the church are houses that date from between these two periods, while the later houses date from the time when quarrying was the mainstay of the villagers.

The Pen-y-ghent Café in the village is a famous walkers' café. It acts as a starting point for the Three Peaks Race, official starting point for walkers completing the Three Peaks Walk and as an unofficial logging in and out point for walkers on the local fells, alerting the authorities if walkers registering their routes and estimated arrival times are overdue.

(2) Drystone Walling

One of the most distinctive and attractive features of the Yorkshire Dales National Park is the drystone walling. It is thought that few such walls existed before the 16th century, but the real acceleration in wall building occurred during the enclosures of the late 18th/early 19th centuries. At that time miles of wall were built up on the high fells, creating the pattern we see today. It is worth remembering that fact on this and other walks in the Dales – the walls you cross are likely to be 200 years old, but are capable of being destroyed in just a few careless seconds.

Wall construction was carried out by skilled builders who could build about a chain (22 yd – about 20 m) of wall in a day. That does not sound a lot, but bear in mind that such a length could involve the moving of 10 tons of stone. To ensure a good level foundation for the wall, trenches would be dug on uneven surfaces. The walls narrow towards the top and are double skinned with occasional tie stones joining the skins for extra strength. The space between the skins was filled with rubble and flat capstones and upright coping stones were then added to protect the skins.

(3) Pen-y-ghent

Many believe that Pen-y-ghent's association with Ingleborough and Whernside means that it is the third highest peak in Yorkshire. In fact it is the fourth highest, the honour of third highest going to Buckden Pike which is all of 8 m (25 ft) higher.

The peak's name, a clear reminder of Celtic Yorkshire, is thought by most experts to derive from the word for 'wind', the same basis as for Castell y Gwynt (Castle of the Winds) on Snowdonia's Glyder range. Pen-y-ghent would then have been the Hill of the Winds. There are, however, those that maintain that the name derives from Pen-y-Cant, the Hill at the Edge, the edge in question being the border of a Celtic tribe.

The peak's distinctive shape results from its being an object lesson in local geology. The peak is a monadnock, an erosional survival. The summit is of Millstone Grit, the main north-south ridge of rocks of the Yoredale Series (shales, sandstone and limestone), the whole sitting on a bed of carboniferous limestone. The stepped outcrops on the south ridge of the peak – the ascent route of the walk – are of resistant Yoredale rock. This mixture of rocks and, therefore, soils makes Pen-y-ghent a marvellous place for the botanist. In April the purple mountain saxifrage (*Saxifraga oppositifolia*) blooms followed, in June, by the yellow mountain saxifrage (*Saxifraga aizoides*) and in July by the white flowers of cloudberry (*Rubus chamaemorus*).

The lover of fine views will also be enthralled by the peak. From the top the sister summits of Ingleborough and Whernside can be seen, and there are marvellous views towards Fountains Fell and Ribblesdale.

(4) Hunt Pot

This pothole is entered through a strangely sinister slot in the limestone. An immediate 27 m (90 ft) drop is followed shortly after by one of 21 m (70 ft). Water flowing into the slot re-emerges at Brants Gill Head, 1.5 km (1 mile) away, just to the north of Horton in Ribblesdale.

(5) Hull Pot

This pothole could hardly be more different from Hunt Pot. Here the sheer 18 m (60 ft) sides of the wide entrance cleft – almost a perfect rectangle measuring 55 × 14 m (180 × 45 ft) – are very picturesque, particularly after heavy rain when a stream pours over them.

Walk 6b Ingleborough

Ingleborough is the most impressive of the Three Peaks, so much so that it seems a pity it is not 13 m (43 ft) taller and, therefore, higher than Whernside. There are many excellent routes to the summit, although the best are that from Clapham, past Gaping Gill, and that from Ingleton, past Crina Bottom. A complete traverse can be made, using the bus to return to the start, but here an alternative, circular route is also suggested.

Walk category: Difficult (4 hours)

Length: 12 km (7.5 miles)

Ascent: 600 m (1970 ft)

Maps: Landranger Sheet 98, Outdoor Leisure Sheet 2

Starting and finishing point: At 745692, the car-park beside the National Park Centre in Clapham.

From the car-park, turn right towards the church (see (1) Clapham) and almost immediately left over a footbridge. Turn right and follow the road beside Clapham Beck. Bear left with the road at the top of the village and, after about 90 m, go right along a walled track signed for Gaping Gill and Ingleborough

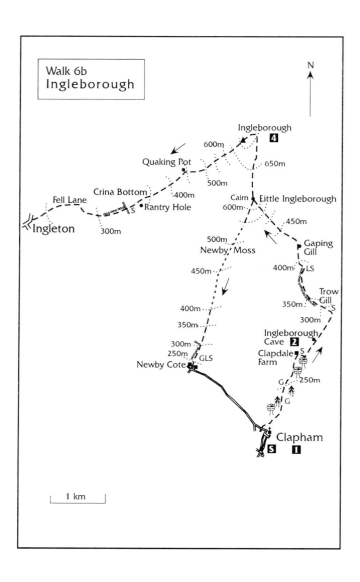

Walk 6b
Ingleborough

N

Ingleborough **4**

600m

650m

Quaking Pot

500m

400m

Cairn Little Ingleborough

Crina Bottom

Fell Lane

600m

450m

Rantry Hole

300m

Ingleton

500m

Gaping Gill

Newby Moss

400m LS

450m

Trow Gill

350m S

300m

400m

350m

Ingleborough Cave **2**

300m

250m GLS

Clapdale Farm

S

Newby Cote

G 250m

G

Clapham **1**

S

1 km

Cave. Follow this gently rising track through two gates to reach
the farm at Clapdale. Go through the farmyard, exiting over a
stile, and turn right to follow a signed path for Ingleborough
Cave. The path drops steeply down to Clapham Beck: turn left
to follow the beck to the cave entrance (see (2) Ingleborough
Cave).

Continue past the cave, going over a footbridge to reach the
narrow and steep-walled, but very attractive, Trow Gill. The
path maintains direction at first, but then bears left with the
gill (a dry valley). Go over a stile to reach an even more
imposing section of the gill, its sheer limestone walls so close
that the gorge is a damp, brooding place. Continue upwards
through the narrowing gorge to reach open ground and continue beside a wall on the left. Ignore the first ladder stile on
the left, bearing right with the wall to reach a second one, close
to a pothole on the right. Cross this stile and follow the clear
path towards the distinctive peak of Ingleborough.

Soon, the wired-off top of Gaping Gill is reached (see (3)
Gaping Gill). Beyond the pothole the path bears left and climbs
to the summit of Little Ingleborough. The descent route to
Clapham goes south from here. Now turn due north for the
final climb to the summit (see (4) Ingleborough). The path
bears to the right of the summit, then swings sharply left to
approach it from the east.

To return to Clapham, reverse the route to Little Ingleborough and bear half-right across Newby Moss, a section of
trackless rough moorland. Maintain a south-south-westerly
line, soon seeing the village of Newby Cote which acts as a
waymarker. Aim for the corner of the first (i.e. last!) field wall
and walk with it on your right, still descending towards the
village. Go over a ladder stile and follow the walled track
beyond to reach a farm and, just beyond, a road. Turn left
along the road to return to Clapham.

For the descent to Ingleton and a bus ride back to Clapham,
maintain direction across the summit plateau and follow the

clear path that descends south-westwards. Follow the path past several potholes and the farm at Crina Bottom (to your right) to reach a ladder stile. Cross to reach a track (Fell Lane) with a wall on the right and an old wall on the left. Soon the track becomes fully enclosed: continue along it until the wall on the right bears away. Now head across the open ground ahead to reach another walled track and follow this to a road. Turn left to reach Ingleton.

(1) Clapham
This is a pretty village, its stone houses spread out along the banks of Clapham Beck. The church, dedicated to St James, was almost completely rebuilt in 1814, retaining only its Perpendicular tower. The earliest church on the site was probably built in the 12th century, but was rebuilt after the battle of Bannockburn when the victorious Scots rampaged through the area, razing the original church. To the north of the village the lake (which is actually called The Lake) is artificial, created by the damming of Clapham Beck by the owner of Ingleborough Hall, the fine old building beyond the church. Reginald Farrer, one of Britain's foremost botanists and an expert on rock plants – he is often called the Father of Rock Gardening – once lived here. He was a member of the Farrer family who owned Ingleborough Hall and estate. The family were responsible for planting the larch, pines and deciduous trees that make Clapham Gill such a lovely place, and for digging the tunnels that allow today's walker access to the fells beyond the estate. It is no surprise that Reginald – who died in 1920 when aged only thirty-nine – became such a lover of plants. Farrer spent a great deal of time in Tibet, Burma and Japan and brought back many previously unknown shrubs and trees to the estate, using them to create a remarkable garden. The garden – which can be visited by following the Ingleborough Estate Trail from Clapham – has around two dozen species of rhododendron as well as other exotic shrubs and a

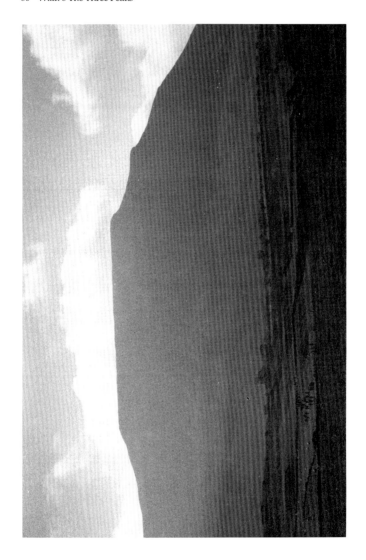

fine alpine garden, many of its plants collected from the European Alps by Reginald Farrer.

Another famous resident of the village was Michael Faraday, the foremost scientist of the early 19th century and, arguably, the greatest experimental scientist of all time. Faraday's father, James, was Clapham's blacksmith.

The village is also the home of *The Dalesman*, a magazine devoted to Yorkshire country life. The magazine was started in the village in 1939.

(2) Ingleborough Cave

The cave is one of only a handful of show caves in the National Park. It was opened in 1838 after the Farrers ordered the smashing of a stalagmite wall about 20 metres (about 70 ft) from the entrance, and the draining of a pool. The public can now explore about 550 m (600 yd) of the cave which has some excellent formations. The tour includes still-active streams and lit pools, these waters being home to shrimps which have lost their colour pigment as it is useless in the darkness of the cave. It is claimed that one of the cave's stalactites is, at 1.5 m (5 ft) the longest free-hanging specimen to have been discovered in Britain.

More experienced cavers have continued the exploration of the system by diving the pool at the cave's end. This exploration has linked the cave to Gaping Gill.

(3) Gaping Gill

This is without doubt the most impressive cave opening in Yorkshire (and, indeed, in Britain), Fell Beck disappearing into the 6 m (20 ft) diameter hole and falling 110 m (360 ft) to the floor of the cave, a drop interrupted only by a ledge – Birkbeck's Ledge, named after one of the cave's early explorers – at approximately half-height. The hole was first descended

Ingleborough from the east

by Edouard-Alfred Martel, the French explorer who is usually credited with having begun the science of speleology. Martel opened many of the huge caves in France's Massif Central and was the first to traverse Provence's Verdon Gorge (taking a route that now bears his name). He was interested in cave hydrology and biology, contributing a great deal to the understanding of cave formation. Martel descended Gaping Gill in August 1895 taking 23 minutes to negotiate the drop.

It is not clear how much Martel learned of the evolution of Gaping Gill, but the walker can gain a clear understanding during the ascent from Clapham. Trow Gill is a dry valley and is likely to have been cut by Fell Beck before the waters of the beck had had time to percolate down through the limestone. Caves form as water percolating downwards, and along fault lines in the limestone, opens larger passages. Linking of these passages creates cave systems, with the stream eventually disappearing underground to flow along a new bed. Ultimately another, lower, passage is created and the stream drops again leaving the upper system dry, just as Trow Gill has been left dry. Sometimes, due to pronounced weaknesses in the rock, large caverns are created underground. If the roof of these is near the surface then it can collapse, creating a huge hole such as here at Gaping Gill.

Originally Fell Beck emerged from underground (the 'official' term for the place where an underground stream emerges is a resurgence) at Ingleborough Cave, but this is now a dry system, the beck's resurgence being Beck Head just below the cave's entrance. As the walker climbs above Gaping Gill other potholes can be seen on the hillside. Ultimately Fell Beck will sink into one of those and the Gaping Gill hole will lose its waterfall.

Those who wish to explore Gaping Gill, but have no particular interest in caving as a sport, can do so at the Spring and August Bank Holidays when local caving clubs set up a winch and bosun's chair to transport visitors up and down. The descent takes about 90 seconds, visitors then seeing Fell Beck disappear again, into the floor of the collapsed chamber. The descent is impressive, the chamber equally so. At 152 m long, 27 m wide and 34 m high (500 × 90 × 110 ft) it is large enough to accommodate York Minster. For full details of the descents, ask at the National Park Centre in Clapham.

(4) Ingleborough

The summit of Ingleborough was the site of the highest hill-fort in England and Wales. The fort, probably Iron Age in origin but possibly earlier, was defended by a stone wall almost 4 m (13 ft) thick. Inside this wall the remains of several circular huts can be made out. Given the nature of the sur-rounding land, which has always offered poor grazing, and the problem of obtaining water, it is likely that the fort was a defensive retreat rather than a permanent village. It was certainly used as a fort during the Brigante revolt against the Romans in the 1st century AD.

From the summit the views are magnificent, taking in the other two of the Three Peaks, Ribblesdale and, to the west, the Forest of Bowland. The panorama dial on the wind shelter helps point out the main features. The shelter and dial were erected in 1953 to celebrate the Coronation of Queen Elizabeth II. The shelter has fared much better than that erected in 1830 by Hornby Roughsedge, a local mill-owner. Roughsedge's shelter was damaged on the day of its official opening when some of the crowd, having brought with them large quantities of local ale, became – how shall we say – high-spirited. The damage was never repaired and the elements soon reduced the shelter to a ruin. Walkers can see this rather sad sight on the edge of the plateau, close to the descent route towards Ingleton.

Walk 6c Whernside

As the highest mountain in the Yorkshire Dales, Whernside is an obvious summit for walkers.

Walk category: Difficult (4 hours)

Length: 13 km (8 miles)

Ascent: 470 m (1540 ft)

Maps: Landranger Sheet 98, Outdoor Leisure Sheet 2

Starting and finishing point: At 765792, near the Station Inn on the B6225, close to its junction with the B6479.

Go northwards along the farm road beside the inn, walking past the viaduct (see (1) Settle to Carlisle Railway) and then bearing right along a path beside the railway. Continue past the Bleamoor Signal Box to reach an aqueduct that crosses the track. Cross the aqueduct and continue along the path beside the stream (with the stream on your left), soon passing the attractive Force Gill waterfall, also on the left. Near the waterfall the path bears right, away from the stream, to follow a fence up Slack Hill. Follow the fence until a stile allows you to cross it. Beyond the stile the path bears left, away from the fence, crossing the moorland of Grain Ings. Follow this path as it bears left around an area of potholes (shake holes) and a tarn (Greensett Tarn), on Greensett Moss, to reach a wall on Whernside's summit ridge. Follow the wall until a stile allows access to the trig. point summit (see (2) Whernside).
   To continue, recross the stile and turn right to follow the ridge wall once more. The striking out point from the ridge can easily be missed, so be cautious: it lies about 1200 m (1300 yd)

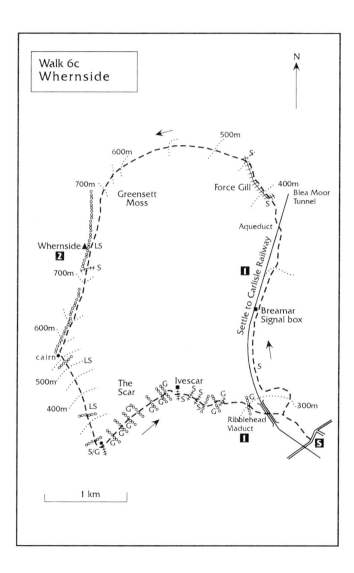

Walk 6c
Whernside

N

500m

600m

700m

Greensett
Moss

Force Gill

S

400m

Blea Moor
Tunnel

Aqueduct

Whernside ▲ LS

2

700m   ‡ S

1

Settle to Carlisle Railway

600m

Breamar
Signal box

cairn •

LS

S

500m

The
Scar

G   Ivescar
G ■
S S
‡ S   G

400m   LS

G

‡

G

S

G

G

G •

300m

S/G ‡

Ribblehead
Viaduct

1

S

1 km

from the summit and is marked by a large cairn at the base of two small, but obvious, patches of scree. It also lies at the closest approach of a wall on your left, where a ladder stile is visible. Turn left at the cairn and make for the ladder stile, crossing it and following the path beyond to another ladder stile.

Cross and descend a field to a third ladder stile. Cross this and turn left through a gate to the right of a barn. Continue ahead, going through another gate to pass a farm, Broadrake, on your left. Maintain direction across several fields linked by gates, with The Scar (over which a waterfall drops) to your left, to reach another farm, Ivescar. Go between the farmhouse and some buildings (using gates and a sheep pen) to reach a large barn. Turn right in front of this barn, then go immediately left through a gate beside it. Bear half-right across the field beyond to a stile. Go over and follow the wall on the left to reach a stile in the corner. Cross this and the field beyond, bearing half-right to reach another stile. Cross this and another field to reach a lane. Turn left, go through a gate and turn right with the lane, following it under the viaduct to reach the outward route. Now reverse the outward route for a few metres to regain the start.

(1) Settle to Carlisle Railway

The line was begun in 1869 by the Midland Railway Company which needed a line linking London, the Midlands and Scotland in order to compete with the west coast line operated by the London and North Western Railway Company and the east coast line operated by the Great Northern Railway Company. The Midland plan was a main line via Derby, but the engineering problems were formidable. The Yorkshire Dales are the worst terrain imaginable for a railway, a series of valleys and high moors that force a line to do exactly what it does not want to do – go uphill and around curves. In the 112 km (70 miles) of track between Settle and Carlisle the railway required fifteen viaducts, twelve tunnels and numerous cuttings. The track took six years to lay and cost £3.5 million – a vast sum for the day and 50 per cent more than the original estimate. The cost of candles during the digging of the Blea Moor Tunnel was £50 per month. But there was also a grimmer price to pay. The line cost many lives, not only through accidents but because of disease, the conditions in which the workers were housed were hopelessly inadequate, the cold and damp combining with a poor diet and fatigue to cause many deaths. The names of those who lost their lives are recorded on tablets in the south porch of Settle Church and the west wall of Chapel-le-Dale Church.

All that remains of the workers' town – called Batty Green, with apparently no sense of irony – can be seen near the viaduct as a series of trenches. Although conditions in the village were harsh, industrial archaeologists are fascinated by Batty Green which seems to have been a genuine 'frontier' town with bars, 'houses of comfort' (to use the euphemism of the time) and chapels. But behind the romance such places can evoke, the truth seems to have been the poor sanitation and regard for welfare that led to the deaths of many who lived there.

The railway created by the hardy inhabitants of Batty Green was one of the finest in the world, and one of the great engineering feats of the 19th century. Occasional suggestions that the line be closed have been greeted with outrage not only by railway enthusiasts but by all who know or have travelled the line. The two best-known features on the line are the Ribblehead Viaduct (originally called the Batty Moss Viaduct and the longest on the line) and the Blea Moor Tunnel, which is also the line's longest, each of which are seen on this walk. The viaduct's statistics are impressive, its twenty-four arches carrying the line 400 m (0.25 mile) at a height of 30 m (100 ft). But as well as being a remarkable piece of engineering the viaduct is also a very attractive work, adding to, rather than

detracting from, the panoramas of the area. The Blea Moor Tunnel, whose entrance is seen from the route – it lies about 350 m north of the aqueduct – is 2.4 km (1.5 miles) long and 150 m (500 ft) below ground at its deepest point.

(2) Whernside

At 736 m (2,415 ft) Whernside is the highest Dales peak. As with the other two of the Three Peaks it owes its existence to the Yoredale Series of rocks which overlay the Great Scar Limestone. Though less attractive than Pen-y-ghent and Ingleborough, the peak is a worthwhile ascent not only as the highest, but for its views and for the possibility of seeing a peregrine falcon. These magnificent birds of prey are successfully re-establishing themselves in Britain after years of persecution and threats from pesticides. Sighting a peregrine is marvellous, particularly if it is 'stooping' for its prey. The 'stoop' is a wings-folded dive which can reach speeds of over 160 k.p.h. (100 m.p.h.) from which the peregrine pulls out when within striking range of its prey, usually a pigeon. Contrary to widely held belief, the peregrine does not strike the pigeon at full speed – that would be risking serious injury – but slows, flattens its flight and takes the pigeon from underneath by plucking it out of the air. If you are lucky enough to see a peregrine, please remember that their survival is still in the balance as a result of egg and chick collectors, and that it is therefore illegal to approach a nest.

The Ribblehead Viaduct and Whernside

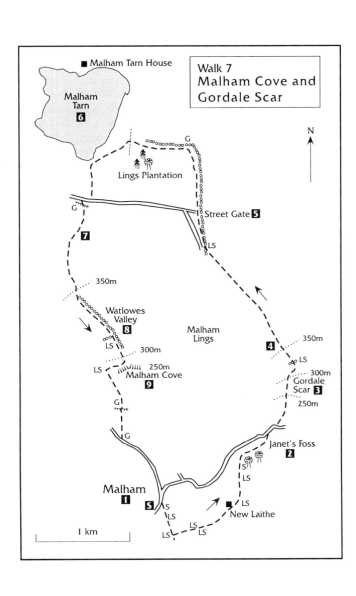

Walk 7
Malham Cove and
Gordale Scar

Malham Tarn House

Malham
Tarn
6

N

Lings Plantation

G

Street Gate **5**

G

LS

7

350m

Watlowes
Valley
8

LS

Malham
Lings

350m

LS

4

300m
Gordale
Scar **3**

250m

300m

LS

250m

Malham Cove
9

G

Janet's Foss
2

S

LS

G

Malham
1

S

LS

LS

LS

New Laithe

LS

LS

LS

LS

1 km

Walk 7 Malham Cove and Gordale Scar

Malham Cove is one of the most impressive features in Britain, but it is just one of several which combine to make this walk a treasure house of geological and scenic wonders. Although neither long nor involving much ascent, the walk is tricky in several places: the climb through Gordale Scar is steep and slippery, the limestone pavement about Malham Cove was apparently constructed to trip the unwary and the Cove itself is sheer. Please take care.

Walk category: Intermediate/Difficult (3 hours)

Length: 11 km (7 miles)

Ascent: 200 m (655 ft)

Maps: Landranger Sheet 98, Outdoor Leisure Sheet 10

Starting and finishing point: At 900627, the National Park Information Centre car-park in Malham.

Turn left from the car-park to reach the main street in Malham (see (1) Malham). Turn right opposite Sparth House to cross a footbridge over the River Aire, then right again to go along a wide path beside the river. The path is both clear and well waymarked from here to Janet's Foss: go over a stile and two ladder stiles, bearing left after the second (close to Mires Barn) to follow a wall – on your left. Use ladder stiles to cross a lane and continue, still with the wall on your left. Beyond the next ladder stile you walk with the wall on your right to reach another

ladder stile. Cross this and the stile ahead to reach a beautiful little gorge and Janet's Foss, to the right (see (2) Janet's Foss).

Continue along the path to reach a road. Turn right for about 90 m then, just after the bridge, turn left along a signed path to Gordale Scar. This section of the walk is paved and it is impossible to lose the way!

The approach to the Scar (see (3) Gordale Scar) is wonderfully impressive, with Gordale Beck bubbling away to the left and the great jaws of rock opening ahead of you. The stepped gorge looks impassable, but as you move closer a devious path up the rocky steps becomes clear. Take care – the rock is wet and slippery, and friable. There is a ladder stile at the top of the gorge: go over this and take the signed path for Malham Tarn. The path follows the edge of the limestone pavement (see (4) Clints and Grykes) that is another of the geological and scenic highlights of the walk.

Follow the path to a ladder stile over a wall. Cross and turn right to reach Street Gate at 905656 (see (5) Street Gate). Continue northwards along a metalled track, with a wall on your right, to reach a cattle grid and gate. Do not go through the gate: instead, turn left and follow a wall (again on your right) to reach a wide crossing track near Lings Plantation. This crossing track is part of the Pennine Way. Do not follow the Way: instead, cross it and bear left towards the edge of Malham Tarn (see (6) Malham Tarn) following a broad path to reach a car-park at 895658.

Turn right along the road, cross Malham Beck and, soon after, turn left through a gate to follow a signed bridleway. The old chimney away to the right from here is all that remains of a 19th century zinc and lead smelter. The path follows the beck, but this soon disappears (see (7) Water Sinks): bear left at a path fork (signed Water Sinks and Malham Cove) and follow the wall on the left for about 900 m, descending to reach

Malham Cove

Watlowes (see (8) Watlowes Dry Valley). Walk through this
narrow valley: the path winds and turns sharply at one point
(by a stile) but is always well defined. At the exit from the
valley, go over a ladder stile to reach the top of Malham Cove
(see (9) Malham Cove). You have now joined the Pennine Way:
turn right along it, following the edge of the Cove. Go over a
ladder stile and follow the Way down the stepped path at the
Cove's western edge. Bear left at the bottom to reach the Cove's
impressive amphitheatre before continuing along the Pennine
Way which goes through a gate and continues easily to a road
(Cove Road). Turn left to return to Malham, walking through
the village to reach the car-park.

(1) Malham

This huddle of stone-built cottages and an old packhorse bridge
is typical of Dales villages, though the tourist development as a
result of the Cove is obvious. Lister's Arms dates from 1723,
while the Buck Inn is much more recent. Lister's changed its
name from Dixon's when it became the property of Thomas
Lister, the first Lord Ribblesdale. The Buck Inn was formerly the
hostel for miners extracting metal ore from the Malham hills.

Today Malham is the most popular village in the National
Park with an excellent Information Centre which provides not
only valuable information on the surrounding area but just
about the only reasonable parking spot in the village. As you
walk through the village admiring the stone cottages, look out
for the dovecotes which once supplied the villagers with their
only meat in winter months, and for the two fine bridges.
Monk's (or New) Bridge near the post office dates from the
17th century (though it was widened a century later) while the
old clapper bridge is at least a century older.

(2) Janet's Foss

The waterfall lies in a delightful wooded gorge occasionally
known as Little Gordale. In local legend Janet was the Queen

of the Fairies and lived behind the waterfall. *Foss* is the Norse word for a waterfall. The fall was formed over a ledge of hard rock, but this has now been covered by a layer of tufa. Tufa is formed when water oversaturated with calcium carbonate – as all the local streams are, after flowing over (and occasionally through) the local carboniferous limestone – deposits the dissolved salt on the material over which it is flowing. In caves, stalactites and stalagmites are created by this process, these formations being a pure form of the calcareous material. In tufa, the deposition is on to a surface that is covered with organic material, such as the algae and mosses that grow in damp environments. These, together with leaves and twigs, become embedded in the deposits, creating a rock that is very friable. If broken, the rock can be seen to be honeycombed, with pieces of embedded vegetation and spaces where the material has decayed.

The beck close to the falls is the home of kingfishers and dippers, while the plant life among the sycamore and ash trees includes dog's mercury, a delicate low plant with an equally delicate greenish flower, and ramsons, a plant with a distinctly less delicate smell – and better known as wild garlic.

(3) Gordale Scar

The limestone of North Yorkshire is a sedimentary rock, laid down below a clear sea in the Carboniferous period of geological time, some 350 million years ago. After the limestone sheet had been raised above the sea the evolutionary processes continued, the stresses in the sheet causing it to split, the southern section dropping by about 1000 m (3280 ft). This split followed a line roughly east-west and is known as the Mid-Craven Fault. Further rocks were deposited beneath a sea lying above the southern section of the limestone sheet, but when these rocks – Bowland Shale and Reef Limestone – were exposed they weathered more quickly than the harder limestone, causing a 'fault-line scarp' to develop. This scarp is a

sharp cliff noticeable to all who drive or walk north to the limestone country around Malham where the roads and paths steepen as they climb the 60 m (200 ft) or so on to the limestone plateau.

The actual creation process of Gordale Scar in the Great Scar Limestone is still debated. Rainwater is slightly acidic due to dissolved carbon dioxide and dissolves carboniferous limestone, particularly along minute cracks and faults in the rock. In time this dissolution process results in streams disappearing underground. Large caverns are created by those underwater streams, producing the cave systems that are such a feature of the area around Ingleborough. Occasionally the underground rivers carve tall, narrow caverns that lie close to the surface and if the cave roof collapses a visible gorge is created, such as that seen at Gordale Scar. The natural arch in the Scar is a remnant of an old roof. On the floor of the newly exposed gorge mosses and lichens took hold, further depositions of calcium carbonate incorporating these into the tufa that once lay across most of the Scar's floor. The passage of countless feet has eroded much of the soft tufa, but sections of it are still visible.

An alternative creation theory is that Gordale Scar was cut by a waterfall formed by meltwater at the end of the last Ice Age. This theory does not seem to be able to explain either the natural arch in the Scar or the tightness of the gorge, but is nevertheless favoured by some geologists.

The Scar is as impressive as Malham Cove but quite different, its huge overhanging walls giving the narrow gorge a dark, cold, almost sinister feel which is a complete contrast to the sunny Cove. Those visitors not familiar with the history of rock climbing in Britain will be amazed to discover that the brooding walls of the Scar are criss-crossed by routes – look forthe flashes of coloured nylon tapes, running belays for leaders on the climbs, some as hard as any in the country.

Drystone walls near Malham Cove

(4) Clints and Grykes

On exposed, flat sheets of limestone rainwater cuts channels at the rock's jointing eventually creating 'grykes', deep fissures, in the rock separated by 'clints', sharp ridges of rock. The bare rock, arid and windblown, offers no hope for plants, but windblown earth collecting in the grykes and mixing with minerals (quartz and clay) dissolved out of the limestone means that enough soil collects for occasional hardy plants to take root and force their way to the surface.

(5) Street Gate

This is the junction of two ancient trackways across the Pennines, the north-south route from Arncliffe to Malham, and the east-west route from Wharfedale to Ribblesdale.

(6) Malham Tarn

In an area of permeable limestone a sheet of water such as this tarn would seem to be a contradiction. The answer is a saucer-shaped intrusion of Silurian slate in the limestone plateau. This slate is impervious to water, the lake forming on it after a natural dam of glacial moraine (also impervious) formed at the end of the last Ice Age. The lake, with a surface area of 62 hectares (153 acres), is one of only two natural lakes in the Dales, the other being Semer Water. The tarn lies at about 370 m (1215 ft) above sea level – making it the highest natural lake in Yorkshire – and frequently freezes in winter.

Malham Tarn is now a Nature Reserve, the Reserve (a Site of Special Scientific Interest for its plant and bird life, the latter visible from a hide at the tarn's north-west corner) encompassing the trees on the northern and eastern shores though these are not natural, having been planted in the 19th century.

On the northern edge of the tarn is Tarn House. Charles Kingsley was staying here when he visited Malham Cove. Seeing the black stripes down the Cove's face he remarked that it looked as if a chimney sweep had fallen down it. That evening, back in the house, that chance remark came back to him and he began to write *The Water Babies*, his most famous work. John Ruskin and Charles Dickens also spent time at the House. It is now owned by the National Trust and houses a Field Studies Centre.

(7) Water Sinks
The dissolving of the limestone plateau by rainwater and run-off from Malham Tarn means that the tarn's outflowing stream disappears here. It resurfaces at Airehead joining the Gordale, Malham and Tranlands Becks to form the River Aire.

(8) Watlowes Dry Valley
The creation of dry valleys in limestone is not well understood, though in the case of Watlowes there appears little doubt that the valley was cut by a stream. There is even a dry waterfall. It is thought that at the end of the Quaternary Ice Age the cracks in the limestone were filled with either remnant ice or with 'till', the ground-up rock that is created below glaciers as they grind remorselessly over their bedrock. Until this ice melted, or the till was washed out, surface-flowing water would have been possible. Eventually the cracks were opened and the water again seeped downwards. Historical records show that in times of extremely heavy and persistent rain a stream has flowed in the Watlowes Valley. While the valley was being created the stream must have flowed over the lip of Malham Cove, creating a truly impressive waterfall.

(9) Malham Cove
This magnificent rock amphitheatre, almost 70 m (230 ft) high and several hundred metres across, is one of the great natural features of Britain. It was formed at the Mid-Craven Fault by glacier and stream action at the end of the last Ice Age, one of the country's most spectacular exhibitions of the power of glaciation. Today the Mid-Craven Fault lies about 400 m south

of the Cove, glacial and stream erosion having cut the lime-stone scarp northwards in the aeons since the fault occurred.

The difference in country between the limestone plateau and the bedrock laid down on top of the limestone after the Mid-Craven Fault dropped the limestone sheet at Malham is best seen from the Cove's lip. Behind you is the sparse vegetation and white outcropped rock of the plateau, while to the south is the thicker, darker green vegetation on the overlying Yoredale Shales and Millstone Grit.

When the stream from the Watlowes Valley was crashing over the Cove it must have been a memorable sight. Today the sheer, and occasionally overhanging, rock walls are home to house martens and rock climbers.

The entrance to Gordale Scar

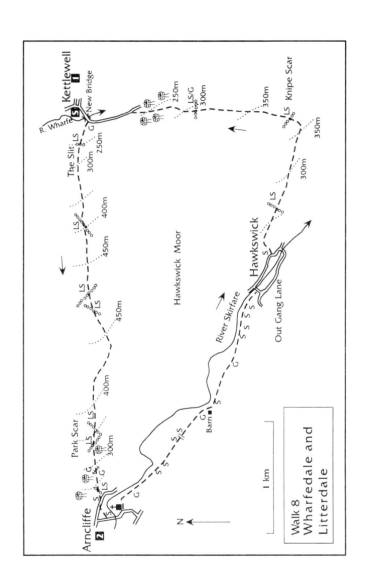

Walk 8
Wharfedale and
Litterdale

1 km

N

Kettlewell
R. Wharfe
New Bridge

The Slit
LS
250m
300m
250m

LS
400m
450m
450m

LS
LS

400m

Park Scar
LS
LS
300m
LS

Arncliffe

G
LS
G
S
S

250m
300m
LS/G
300m

350m
Knipe Scar
350m

300m
LS

Hawkswick Moor

Hawkswick
S
Out Gang Lane

River Skirfare

S S S
G

G
Barn
S
S/S
S S
G

Walk 8 Wharfedale and Littondale

South of Kettlewell, which lies in Wharfedale, the River Wharfe is joined by the River Skirfare which flows through Littondale. The prow-shaped ridge of high moor that separates the two dales offers excellent walking and some of the best views in the National Park. This route crosses and then recrosses the ridge, obtaining the best of the views and visiting both dales.

Walk category: Intermediate (3.5 hours)

Length: 11 km (7 miles)

Ascent: 500 m (1640 ft)

Maps: Landranger Sheet 98, Outdoor Leisure Sheets 10 and 30

Starting and finishing point: At 968723, the car-park beside the River Wharfe in Kettlewell.

From the car-park, return to the road and turn away from the village (see (1) Kettlewell), soon crossing the New Bridge over the River Wharfe. Now turn right along a signed path for Arncliffe, soon bearing left away from the main path to reach a ladder stile over a wall. The stile is waymarked with a yellow disc: these waymarkers are followed throughout the route. The path heads upwards towards the scar, using an improbable gap (The Slit) in the rocks to ascend to the moor above. Here, the yellow waymarkers lead to a footpath sign. Maintain direction beyond the sign, then bear slightly right to reach a ladder stile over a wall. Cross this and bear left. The path eases away from the wall, then bears right towards the scar. On this section there are superb views into Wharfedale to the right.

Climb the scar and cross a ladder stile in the wall ahead, following the path beyond to another ladder stile. Maintain direction beyond this – the yellow waymarkers give the line when the path is faint – heading slightly downhill to reach another footpath sign. There, bear right, and continue to descend into Littondale. Go through a wall gap, bearing left beyond it to reach another footpath sign. Maintain direction to reach a ladder stile over a wall. Cross this and continue ahead to reach another. Cross and follow a path steeply down through Park Scar and the wood beyond.

Descend through the wood, going through a gate and continuing to reach a ladder stile. Cross and continue ahead to another stile on to a lane. Go straight across and descend to the edge of the River Skirfare. Turn right beside the river to reach a road. Turn left and cross the river into Arncliffe (see (2) Arncliffe). Bear left to pass the church (on your left) and then go left again along the drive to the old vicarage, following a signed path for Hawkswick. The path goes through the vicarage yard: please be restrained when viewing the house, it is privately owned.

This path is followed all the way to the hamlet of Hawkswick, using stiles and gates to link fields beside the River Skirfare. At first the path stays close to the water's edge, but as the river swings away the path maintains direction (there is a stile across the wall on your right: cross and bear left across the field to the stile opposite), reaching the riverbank again close to a barn. The river then bends away again, but is reached beyond further fields, the path then staying close to it to reach a bridge.

There is a choice of routes here, with little to choose between them: either go left, across the river, and turn right along the road into Hawkswick hamlet. There, turn left along a signed footpath for Kettlewell, following it to a stile. Cross this and follow the path beyond uphill. The alternative route goes right to reach a road (Out Gang Lane) and turns left along it. Follow the road over the river to reach a t-junction. Go straight across and along the track opposite, bearing right to follow a wall uphill. The two routes join here.

Go over the stile ahead and continue with the wall on your right, passing below Knipe Scar, on the left. Maintain direction to reach a footpath sign, continuing ahead to reach a prominent cairn. There, turn sharp left to reach a ladder stile over a wall. The views into both Littondale and Wharfedale are excellent on this section of the walk. Cross the ladder stile and bear left across the brow of the ridge. Beyond the brow Kettlewell comes into view: go through an old wall and continue to reach a ladder stile. Cross this and continue to a gate and ladder stile at the next wall. Go through or over and follow the path beyond which goes along the edge of a small wood before descending steeply through it to reach a road. Turn left along the road to return to the start.

(1) Kettlewell

Named for Ketel, a Norse chieftain, the village achieved prominence in medieval times when the abbeys of Coverham and Fountains, and Bolton Priory all had estates here, the produce from these estates being sold at the village market. Later, water from the Wharfe powered lead smelters and cloth mills. Today tourism is the mainstay, visitors using the village as a centre for exploring Wharfedale and such local highspots as the overhanging Kilnsey Crag, one of the Dales' most distinctive features. St Mary's, the village church, was built in 1820 – though much restored half a century later – to replace a Norman church which had been demolished the previous year. The font, decorated with the crest of the Percy family, is all that survives from the Norman building.

The New Bridge which the walk uses to cross the Wharfe hardly merits the name, though it has been restored since it

was first built to replace the ford. Look carefully for the original masons' marks on the stonework.

(2) Arncliffe

The village – its name deriving from the Norse for 'eagle cliff' – is the largest in Littondale. It is a very picturesque place, its houses seeming to melt into the hillside, and achieved fame as the original setting for the television series *Emmerdale Farm*. The series' name derived from Amerdale, the original name for Littondale. Such media fame was in keeping with local history: Charles Kingsley, the author of *The Water Babies* and *Westward Ho!*, was an occasional visitor to Old Cotes, a 17th century house near Bridge End. The inspiration for *The Water Babies* was Malham Cove, but the section where Tom, the sweep, escapes across limestone country was very clearly inspired by Littondale close to Arncliffe. The village church, dedicated to St Oswald, dates from the mid-18th century, though it retains its 15th century tower. Bishop John Robinson, the author of *Honest to God*, a controversial book in its day, is buried in the churchyard.

Knipe Scar

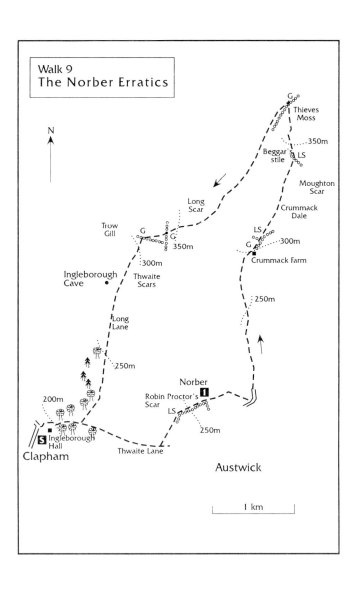

Walk 9
The Norber Erratics

N

Thieves
Moss
G
350m
Beggar's
stile
LS

Moughton
Scar

Crummack
Dale

Long
Scar

Trow
Gill
G
G
350m
300m

LS
G
300m
Crummack Farm

Ingleborough
Cave

Thwaite Scars

250m

Long
Lane

250m

200m

Norber
1

Robin Proctor's
Scar
LS
250m

Ingleborough
Hall
S
Clapham

Thwaite Lane

Austwick

1 km

Walk 9 The Norber Erratics

The Erratics, reminders of the last Ice Age, are one of the most appealing of the many fine geological features of the Dales. This walk visits the boulders and then continues into Crummack Dale to explore a limestone pavement that is the equal of the more famous one at Malham. There are also superb views of Ingleborough and Pen-y-ghent.

Walk category: Intermediate (3 hours)

Length: 11 km (7 miles)

Ascent: 375 m (1230 ft)

Maps: Landranger Sheet 98, Outdoor Leisure Sheet 2

Starting and finishing point: At 745692, the car-park in Clapham beside the National Park Centre.

Turn right from the car-park, following the road towards the church in Clapham (see Note (1) to Walk 6b). Just before the church, where the road goes left, turn right along a lane, going between the church and Ingleborough Hall (to the right). Follow the lane through two short, but dark, tunnels. The tunnels were built at the same time as the Hall (in about 1840) to give the Hall owners access to their woodland – using the tunnels as bridges – while keeping the users of the bridleway (which the route follows) off their land and, presumably, out of sight.

About 500 m beyond the tunnels, ignore the turning to the left, Long Lane (the return route), continuing ahead along Thwaite Lane. Go past a small infant wood on the right (Summit Clump), continuing for a further 800 m (0.5 mile) to reach a signed footpath for Norber on the left. Go over the ladder stile and turn half-right along the path beyond, heading towards the prominent Robin Proctor's Scar and a wall elbow. The Norber Erratics are the grey boulders scattered beneath the Scar, the walk tracing a route between them for the next several hundred metres (see (1) Norber Erratics).

Go around the wall elbow, following the wall (on your right) to a ladder stile. Cross and continue along the wall, but where it turns sharp right, maintain direction to reach a signpost. The best of the erratics are to the left from here, but after exploring you will need to return to the signpost. Go over the ladder stile ahead and turn half-left to reach the end of the wall on the right. There, turn right and follow the wall on the left to reach a lane. Turn left and follow the lane all the way to Crummack Farm, a distance of about 2 km (1.25 miles). At the farm, maintain direction, with a wall on your immediate right and the farm further away on the right. Go over a ladder stile and continue along the path which bears left, away from the wall on the right.

The path climbs gently into the head of Crummack Dale, reaching a path fork below Moughton Scar. Take the right branch, soon reaching a ladder stile (Beggar's Stile) over a short section of wall that bridges a gap in the Scar. Cross and turn left along the wall, then bear right across the superb limestone pavement (see Note (4) to Walk 7). At the pavement's end, maintain direction across a shallow valley to reach a gate in a wall. Go through and turn left along a track beside the wall (i.e. with it on your left). Continue along the track when it bears right, away from the wall. Ignore a path leading off left,

A Norber Erratic

maintaining direction past two cairns and going over at a path junction to reach a fork. Take the right branch, descending towards a wall elbow. There, maintain direction to reach a gate in a wall. Go through and maintain direction to reach another gate in the wall opposite. Beyond this is Long Lane, a walled lane that leads back towards Clapham. Follow the lane, passing Ingleborough Cave, to the right (see Note (2) to Walk 6b), to reach its t-junction with Thwaite Lane, the junction passed on the outward route. Turn right and reverse the outward route back to the start.

(1) Norber Erratics

Although glaciers usually grind up the rock surface over which they move, depositing the material as lateral or terminal moraine, they occasionally pluck out and carry large chunks of rock. Such boulders can be carried some distance, and if the glacier then retreats the boulder is left remote from its point of origin. Until the Ice Age and glacier movements were understood (which occurred only about 150 years ago with some pioneering work by the Swiss glaciologist Louis Agassiz) such boulders were a mystery to geologists who called them 'erratics'. The Norber Erratics are of dark grey Silurian gritstone and were picked up from Crummack Dale where this rock lies at the surface. Interestingly the point of origin is actually below the present position of the boulders, so that they have not only been moved horizontally, but uphill as well. Only recently has the ability of glaciers to have an uphill component to their downhill flow been understood. Some of the boulders now sit on 'stools' of limestone, these white supports accentuating the difference between the rock types. Such perched boulders are, surprisingly, a comparatively common feature of erratics. Normally this is due to the boulder being deposited on a column of moraine, but here that is clearly not the mechanism. The supports are actually attached to the bedrock, the erosion of softer sections of the limestone having created the stool-like effect. The height of the stools now gives a measure of the rate of erosion since the Ice Age, as the boulders would have been dropped on to the limestone sheet. That rate works out at 1 cm every 200 years.

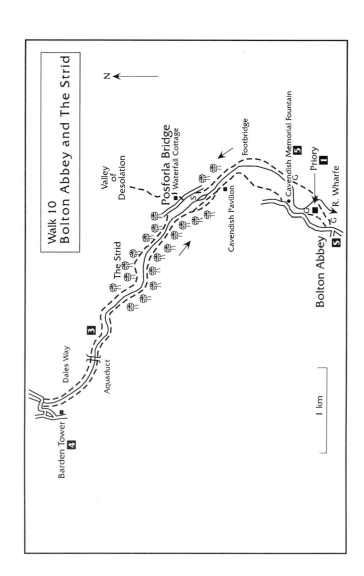

Walk 10
Bolton Abbey and The Strid

N

Barden Tower **4**

Dales Way

Aquaduct

3

The Strid

Valley
of
Desolation

Posforla Bridge
■ Waterfall Cottage

Footbridge

Cavendish Pavillion

Cavendish Memorial Fountain
G
Priory **1**
5

R. Wharfe

Bolton Abbey **S7**

1 km

Walk 10 Bolton Abbey and The Strid

Bolton Priory is one of Britain's most romantic ruins, and inspired a famous painting by J. M. W. Turner. From it an inspiring walk follows the Wharfe to The Strid where the river is crammed into a narrow gorge through which it rushes in great style. But though it is an attractive spot, it is also a dangerous one and great care is needed on the short sections of the walk that approach it. The rest of the walk is straightforward and on easy paths, the classification reflecting the passage of The Strid.

Most of this walk is along permissive paths: please obey the Country Code so that future access is not prejudiced.

Walk category: Intermediate/Difficult (3 hours)

Length: 12 km (7.5 miles)

Ascent: 50 m (165 ft)

Maps: Landranger Sheet 98, Outdoor Leisure Sheet 10

Starting and finishing point: At 071539, the car-park at Bolton Abbey.

From the car-park, turn left, towards the village, soon passing the road to Burnsall (the B6160, to the left). Beyond this, and the post office to the right, turn right through a gate and follow a footpath signed for the priory. The ruins of Bolton Priory, to the left, are soon passed (see (1) Bolton Priory). Follow the path to a footbridge over the River Wharfe. Cross and turn left along the riverbank. Soon, at a path junction, turn right up steps and follow the path beyond, crossing one stile, to reach a road. There are marvellous views of the Wharfe and the priory ruins on this section of the walk.

Turn left along the road to reach a ford. Cross the stream – there is a footbridge to the right – and almost immediately go left along a path, soon reaching a stile on the right. Cross this and follow the path beyond to reach a stile on to a road. The road leads (leftwards) to the Cavendish Pavilion café which is passed on the return route. Cross the road and the stile opposite and follow the path beyond through fine woodland to reach a road. A turn right here follows a 3.5 km (2 miles) detour to the Valley of Desolation. (Go along the road, then left just beyond Waterfall Cottage. The path leads to the Valley: return along the same route). The valley's name is said to derive from the devastation wrought by a storm in 1826. That seems long enough ago to explain why the name is no longer appropriate for such a beautiful little valley.

Our route turns left, crossing Posforth Bridge over an infeed stream of the Wharfe. Just beyond the bridge, turn left along a path that hugs the riverbank as it heads towards The Strid (see (2) The Strid). The footpath down to The Strid itself is closed at present, a diverted path going above the gorge. This is a safer option, but misses the real drama of the scene. The Strid can still be reached by short paths, but the gorge must be approached with caution: the paths close to it are rocky and slippery and need care. The diverted path soon reaches the riverbank again, following it through more excellent woodland. Go over a stile and continue along the riverbank to reach a turreted Victorian aqueduct. The walk can be shortened here, crossing the aqueduct and turning left along the opposite riverbank, but it is best to continue along the path, crossing two more stiles to reach a gate on to a road. This section of the walk follows the Dales Way (see (3) Dales Way). Turn left to cross Barden Bridge, an elegant structure which, as the inscription notes, was reconstructed in 1676 at the expense of the whole West Riding.

Just beyond the bridge, go left over a stile to reach the riverbank, with Barden Tower up on the right (see (4) Barden Tower). Follow the riverbank back to the aqueduct, where the Dales Way is rejoined, continuing to reach a gate into Strid Wood, a Site of Special Scientific Interest notable for its plant and bird life. The next section of the walk is on a permissive path through the Devonshire Estate and a small charge is made (collected at a hut near the Cavendish Pavilion).

Beyond the gate, follow the path that stays closest to the river to reach The Strid again. Here, too, the path is slippery and great care is needed on the traverse of the gorge. Beyond, the path is much easier, passing through beautiful Strid Wood. At a path junction, close to an island in the centre of the river, either branch can be taken, the two paths rejoining close to the Cavendish Pavilion. From the café, continue beside the river, going through the car-park/picnic site (an alternative start for the walk). At the car-park's end, bear half-right, away from the river to reach a road and a memorial (see (5) Cavendish Memorial). Turn left along the road, then left again through a gate to reach the priory ruins. Follow the drive past the ruins to regain the road, going along it to reach a t-junction. Turn left to return to the start.

(1) Bolton Priory
William the Conqueror granted land in this part of the Yorkshire Dales to the de Romilly family one of whom, Alicia, established an Augustinian priory here in 1154, moving the canons from an established priory at Embsay about 7 km (4 miles) to the west. The site had previously been occupied by a Saxon manor house. Although a reasonably wealthy foundation, Bolton Priory took centuries to build. Indeed, by the time of its dissolution in 1539 the western front and tower of the church had still not been completed. The nave of the church is

now the parish church of the village of Bolton Abbey and is worth visiting for its stained glass and paintings. The fact that the village is Bolton Abbey while the monastic house were Bolton Priory reflects the fact that differences between Cistercian, Benedictine and Augustinian houses were sometimes lost on the layman. To add to the confusion, the church is officially the Priory Church of Bolton Abbey.

Of the priory, little remains apart from the ruins of the chancel. These romantic ruins have long attracted visitors and artists, visits becoming very popular after Edwin Landseer painted *Bolton Abbey in Olden Times* in the early years of the 19th century.

Bolton Hall, which incorporates the old priory gatehouse, is a residence of the Dukes of Devonshire. The Old Rectory, to the south of the priory, was built in 1700 with money left in the will of Robert Boyle who died in 1691. Boyle was born in Lismore Castle, Ireland, the son of the Earl of Cork, and became one of the foremost scientists of the age. He is most famous for Boyle's Law relating the volume and pressure of a gas, but in the curious way of the scientists of that period also spent time attempting to turn base metals into gold, being a believer in alchemy. Boyle was deeply religious and left the money in his will to his nephew, the Earl of Burlington, to be used for charitable purposes. Despite the house's name, the Earl actually built it as a school which it was until 1874 when it became the rectory.

(2) The Strid

Here the River Wharfe is confined to a rocky gorge that, at its narrowest, is little more than 2 metres (6.5 ft) wide, a restriction that causes it to foam and rage, the water having worn the rocks smooth. The name derives from the 'stride' that could be taken over the gorge, though this is not recommended: several

The Strid

people have failed to make the step and death has been the inevitable result of those failures.

(3) Dales Way
The fine 130 km (81 mile) walk links Ilkley with Bowness-on-Windermere, tracing a route through the dales of Yorkshire and the Lake District.

(4) Barden Tower
The tower is one of several lodges built originally in the 12th century as hunting lodges or houses for forest keepers. When the land was inherited by Henry, Lord Clifford in the late 15th century he rebuilt and extended it, using it as one of his main residences. Clifford was known locally as the Shepherd Lord as he had been brought up as the son of a shepherd. Young Henry had been born at the height of the Wars of the Roses and his mother, fearing for his safety, fostered him to the shepherd rather than risk having him murdered. Only when he was thirty-two, after the battle of Bosworth, did Henry inherit the estate. As he had never been tutored, the monks of Bolton Priory were requested to give him a crash course in learning, but despite becoming an accomplished scholar Henry preferred the simple life to that of his aristocratic neighbours, living in the tower in preference to his more palatial residence at Skipton.

The tower fell into disrepair, but was renovated in the 17th century by a later member of the family, Lady Anne Clifford. Lady Anne's father was the Lord, but as she was his only child he willed the estate to his brother and his brother's son. Lady Anne fought the will for many years, but only received her rightful inheritance when her cousin died childless. She then restored the tower and lived in it until her death, aged eighty-six, in 1676. Sadly the tower is now once more ruinous. Beside it stands an old priest's house and chapel, also the work of the Cliffords. When it was no longer required, the building was converted into a farmhouse. It has now been converted again, this time into an excellent restaurant. The nearby barn – a 'shippon' in the local dialect – is now a bunkhouse for weekend walkers looking for basic accommodation.

(5) Cavendish Memorial

Frederick Charles Cavendish, born in 1836, the son of the Duke of Devonshire, was made Chief Secretary of Ireland by William Gladstone, then the Prime Minister, in 1882. Cavendish landed in Dublin on 6 May and immediately went for a walk in Phoenix Park with his under-secretary. The pair were set upon by a gang of 'Invincibles', an extremist Irish group, and stabbed to death. Cavendish's murder prevented any progress on efforts to solve the problems of Irish separatism for many years and shocked the inhabitants of the West Riding where public subscription paid for the erection of this covered fountain as a memorial.

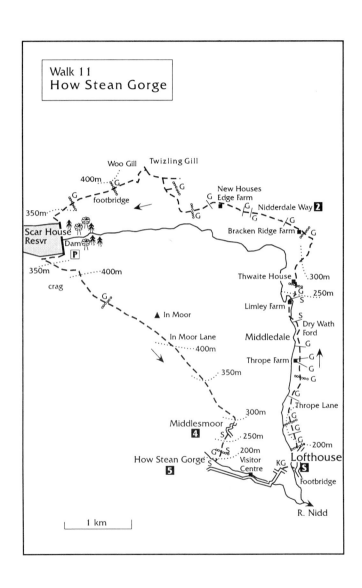

Walk 11
How Stean Gorge

Woo Gill   Twizling Gill

400m
G
footbridge   G
350m   G
New Houses
Edge Farm
G
Nidderdale Way **2**
G
Scar House
Resvr
Dam
P
G   Bracken Ridge Farm   G

350m   400m
crag   Thwaite House   300m
G   G   250m
S
▲ In Moor   Limley Farm
S   Dry Wath
In Moor Lane   Middledale   Ford
400m   G
Thrope Farm   G
350m   G
G

300m   G
Middlesmoor   Thrope Lane
4   G
S   250m   G
G   S   200m   G   200m
How Stean Gorge   G   S   Lofthouse
5   Visitor   KG   **S**
Centre   Footbridge

R. Nidd

1 km

Walk 11 How Stean Gorge

Nidderdale is one of the wildest and least visited of the Yorkshire Dales. Its upper reaches have been flooded to produce two large reservoirs, but the section from Lofthouse to the first of these, Scar House Reservoir, is superb country. This route follows the northern loop of the Nidderdale Way which explores the upper valley before crossing In Moor to reach Middlesmoor and the spectacular How Stean Gorge. The gorge itself can only be visited after paying a fee, but is well worth the outlay.

Walk category: Difficult (4 hours)

Length: 16 km (10 miles)

Ascent: 400 m (1310 ft)

Maps: Landranger Sheet 99, Outdoor Leisure Sheet 30

Starting and finishing point: At 101735, the car-park in the centre of Lofthouse. An alternative start is at 069767, the car-park at the Scar House Reservoir. This is reached by a toll road from Lofthouse: take the road for Middlesmoor and Stean, but soon turn right along the reservoir access road. A third alternative is the car-park at How Stean Gorge. This is less satisfactory as visitors to the gorge may not be able to tear themselves away in order to follow the walk.

From the car-park, head north through the village (see (1) Lofthouse) , following the Nidderdale Way (see (2) Nidderdale

Way), along the road to Masham. As the road bears right and starts to ascend towards Lofthouse Moor, go straight on along a track, Thrope Lane, still heading northwards. Go through a gate and follow the track past Thrope Farm to reach the Dry Wath ford. Cross the ford and go through a gate on to a path. Follow the path to a stile. Cross and continue along the path to reach a red-girdered barn at Limley Farm. Pass the barn on your left and go through the farmyard, bearing right and then left to reach a path that descends to the river. Cross and go through a gate.

Go past a barn to reach a track that rises steeply to reach a gate into Thwaite House, once a grange of Fountains Abbey. Go through the gate on the left of the buildings and follow the enclosed path beyond which soon curves left (north-west-wards) to reach Bracken Ridge Farm. Go through a gate and bear right along the drive to reach a track beside a wall, on your left. This is The Edge, a terrace of moorland, with a steep moorland edge on the right and fine views to both the left and ahead. Follow the terrace track to New Houses Edge Farm, passing several other buildings on the way.

Go past the farm and cross another ford (over an infeed of the River Nidd) to reach a path fork. The branch to the left descends to the river, but we head straight on (still on Nidder-dale Way), the path contouring along the hillside and passing a clump of woodland, to the left, before turning sharp right to follow the valley of another Nidd infeed stream steeply uphill.

Go through a gate, then head for a wall. Here a path offering cream teas goes left, but the route bears right (towards a white post) to reach a track coming in from the right. Turn left along this track. This short section of the walk is not as on the OS Outdoor Leisure Sheet, breaking right earlier, but is very clear on the ground.

Bear left with the track, crossing the delightfully named Twizling Gill. Cross the equally delightfully named Woo Gill, then bear right across open moor. Go past Firth Plantation, to the left, then through a gate; follow the path beyond through boggy ground and several gates to reach the track from the dam of Scar House Reservoir (see (3) Nidderdale Reservoirs).

Turn left along the track and cross the dam. Turn right along the road beside the water, then go left up a track (In Moor Lane). Follow this rough lane steeply upwards. Beyond a gate the track starts to descend, though it remains rough: follow it to reach the road in Middlesmoor (see (4) Middlesmoor). Follow the road through the village, passing the church, to your left. The road goes steeply downhill as it leaves the village: follow the road around a left bend and then take the path on the right, following it downhill towards How Stean Gorge (see (5) How Stean Gorge). The gorge can no longer be entered at this end, the route crossing it to reach a road on the far side. Turn left along the road to reach the entrance to the gorge (together with a car-park and café) on your left. A small fee is payable before the gorge can be explored. After exploring, return to the road and turn left along it, heading towards Lofthouse and soon crossing a bridge over How Stean Beck. Follow the road past a turn to Middlesmoor, on the left, then, at a layby, go left through a kissing gate and follow the path beyond between a barn and a cricket pitch to reach another kissing gate. Go through, cross the road to the reservoirs and continue to a footbridge over the River Nidd. Cross and follow the path back into Lofthouse.

(1) Lofthouse

This pretty little village was the site of the last station on the Nidd Valley Light Railway, opened in 1907 to carry equipment for the construction of the Nidderdale reservoirs. The line was owned by Bradford Corporation, a unique example in Britain of what would be called a local council (rather than a private company or the state) owning a railway. Sadly this form of public ownership could not sustain the railway. After the reservoirs had been completed the line was kept open for the

residents of Nidderdale and visitors to the dale and How Stean Gorge, but eventually closed in 1936.

(2) Nidderdale Way

This 80 km (50 mile) route explores Nidderdale from its fertile, lowland meadows to the open moor at the dale's head. The walk described here follows the Way on its loop around the high moor. The Way is reasonably well signed throughout its route with yellow arrows and the occasional inscribed post.

(3) Nidderdale Reservoirs

There are actually three reservoirs in Nidderdale, the Gouthwaite lying beside the main dale road between Ramsgill and Wath. Gouthwaite was the first of the three to be completed, in 1901, the highest of the three, Angram, was completed after World War I. Beneath the waters of Angram lies a former grange of Bylands Abbey. Before the water rose it had been the highest farm in Nidderdale. Scar House Reservoir, whose dam is walked on this route, was completed in 1936. At that time the dam was the largest stone dam in Europe. When the Yorkshire Dales National Park boundary was drawn in 1954, Nidderdale was excluded. This could hardly be justified on the grounds that the dale was lacking in natural beauty, despite its having been one of the most industrialized of the dales, with linen manufacturing from locally grown flax and lead mining above The Edge. It was, in fact, due to official horror that walkers and other undesirables might pollute Bradford's water if they were allowed close to the reservoirs. When the lunacy of this policy was recognized, the road giving access to the reservoirs for maintenance purposes was opened to the public and the surrounding area was designated an Area of Outstanding Natural Beauty. Today, as walkers will note, there is a car-

Scar House Reservoir

park and picnic area at the southern end of the Scar House dam, the car-park offering an alternative start for the walk.

(4) Middlesmoor

Perched at the top of a steep hill in as windswept a position as could be imagined, Middlesmoor is far more attractive than might be thought. The church is dedicated to St Chad, a 7th century saint who preached at the Saxon cross now housed inside the church.

(5) How Stean Gorge

The gorge is a picturesque and exciting spot, an 800 m ravine up to 25 m (80 ft) deep which is explored by suspension bridges and rock ledges. As with the other tight gorges of the Yorkshire Dales, How Stean is a botanist's paradise, with mosses, liverworts and ferns in abundance and clusters of oak, ash and other deciduous trees.

Walk 12 Swaledale and Tan Hill

No book of walks in the Yorkshire Dales would be complete without a route in Swaledale. The dale is wild and remote, and considered by many to be the finest of all. Our route starts in Upper Swaledale, leaving it to follow the Pennine Way to the Tan Hill Inn, the highest in England. On its return from Tan Hill the route crosses high, boggy moor with few landmarks and occasionally difficult route finding. If you are not absolutely convinced of your ability with map and compass, it is best to wait for a dry day with good visibility.

Walk category: Difficult (4.5 hours)

Length: 18 km (11.25 miles)

Ascent: 350 m (1150 ft)

Maps: Landranger Sheet 98, Outdoor Leisure Sheet 30

Starting and finishing point: At 893013, in the village of Keld. There is a car-park at the bottom of the village and parking is also possible near the toilet block at the village entrance. It is also possible to start the walk from the Tan Hill Inn.

From Keld (see (1) Swaledale) take the track which heads south-eastwards beside the church (signposted for Muker), and follow it for about 300 m, going through a gate, to its junction with the Pennine Way. The track ahead has brought the Way from Thwaite: turn left and cross a footbridge to follow the Way north towards Tan Hill. Beyond the bridge, bear left, then

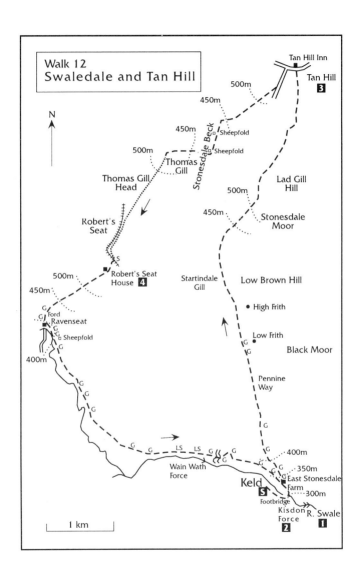

Walk 12
Swaledale and Tan Hill

N

Tan Hill Inn
Tan Hill
3

500m

450m

Stonesdale Beck

450m
Sheepfold

450m
Sheepfold

500m
Thomas
Gill

Thomas Gill
Head

500m

Lad Gill
Hill

500m

450m
Stonesdale
Moor

Robert's
Seat

S

500m
Robert's Seat
House **4**

450m

Startindale
Gill

Low Brown Hill

• High Frith

G
Ford
Ravenseat

G
G
G
Sheepfold
G

• Low Frith

G
G

Black Moor

400m

G

G

G

Pennine
Way

G

G
G
LS   LS   G   G
G
G

Wain Wath
Force

G

400m

G   350m
G
G East Stonesdale
Farm

Keld

S

300m

Footbridge

Kisdon
Force
2

R. Swale
1

1 km

right (with East Gill Force waterfall close by on the right), to reach a farm track. Here the Pennine Way crosses the Coast-to-Coast Walk. To the right, along the Walk, is the Kisdon Force waterfall on the River Swale (see (2) Kisdon Force), a detour of about 800 m (0.5 mile) there and back.

Our route follows the Pennine Way up the farm track to East Stonesdale Farm. Here the Coast-to-Coast Walk bears away to the left – this is the return route – the Pennine Way following an enclosed lane northwards to reach a gate on to the moor (Black Moor). Now maintain direction across the moor, passing to the left of Low Frith Farm and High Frith Farm (though these cannot be seen until you have climbed higher up the moor). The Pennine Way is running parallel to Startindale Gill, to your left, which is fed by a series of streamlets occasionally crossed by plank bridges (put there for farm vehicles rather than walkers). Just beyond the head of the gill, and close to the moorland road which links Swaledale with Tan Hill, to the left, the Way bears right to reach an unnamed gill and, beyond, Lad Gill, both of which are wider streams. These gills are forded, but this can prove tricky after prolonged or heavy rain. If it is impossible, a detour to the road must be made, returning to the far side of the streams.

Continue along the Pennine Way, climbing Stonesdale Moor and Lad Gill Hill, then crossing to Tan Hill where the evidence of mining is all around (see (3) Tan Hill). Some of the air shafts on the moor are deep and unprotected, and should be approached with caution or not at all. As Wainwright says in his *Pennine Way Companion*, Tan Hill is no place to walk in the dark. Continue through the minefield to reach the Tan Hill Inn (see (3) Tan Hill).

From the inn, go westwards along the road (i.e. turn left as you approach the inn), soon reaching a crossroads. Turn left again, going along the road for Keld for about 250 m to reach a signed path for Ravenseat, on the right. Take this path, which soon becomes somewhat indistinct, heading south-westwards (i.e. bearing left at equally indistinct junctions) and walking parallel to Tan Gill, on your left. The path is an old 'jagger' or coal road. The path passes a forlorn signpost, then reaches the junction of two sikes and another signpost. Turn left to follow Stonesdale Beck (with the beck on your right), passing an old sheepfold, over on the right. At the next sheepfold ruin (also on the right) a signpost points the way up Thomas Gill. Cross the stream and walk uphill, with the stream on your right, towards a signpost seen on the ridge ahead.

At the signpost turn left and follow the ridge-top path. The path soon becomes indistinct and can be easily lost. The easiest way is to bear towards the boundary fence, uphill and to the right, and to turn left to follow it, the fence finding the best way through the boggy ground of Robert's Seat. Stay with the fence when it turns sharp left to reach a stile. Cross and follow the more distinct path beyond to reach the ruin of Robert's Seat House (see (4) Robert's Seat House) and the curious sight of a TV aerial planted in the middle of the moor.

The path soon reaches a signpost which points the way to a stile over a fence. Now follow yellow-topped posts, with Bryclose Gutter to the left, to reach a gate/stile. Cross and descend to a ford. Negotiate the ford to reach the farm at Ravenseat. Go past the barns and bear left (heading south-eastwards) in front of the house to reach a footbridge. The route now follows signs and yellow paint splashes between buildings and on through several gates to reach two more buildings. The route is now well defined, passing an old house and continuing through several gates and wall gaps to reach a ladder stile over a wall. Cross this and another ladder stile further on, then bear left at an indistinct fork to reach a road.

Cross the road and follow the drive to East Stonesdale Farm. At the farm, go through a gate and turn right to reverse the outward route back to the starting point in Keld.

(1) Swaledale

Swaledale's remoteness and wildness seem to give it a character all of its own, the unfenced roads and moors reminiscent of a time before tourists – perhaps even settlers – came this way. This feeling of an ancient landscape is helped by the place-names which are almost all derived directly from Old Norse. Keld, where we start the walk, means a 'spring', Thwaite means a 'forest clearing' and Muker means a 'narrow field'. *Saetr*, meaning a shieling or hill pasture, crops up in Ravenseat (Rafn's Saetr) and Gunnerside (Gunnar's Saetr). In its early stages the walk goes through Shot Lathe: Lathe is from *llatha*, a Norse building constructed at the top of a field. It had two storeys, a hayloft sitting above the cattle byre. Even the more common names, gill, beck, moss and fell, are Old Norse.

The dale's remoteness – added to its harsh winters: look at how the village houses are carefully arranged to gain the maximum shelter for all the villagers – led to the breeding of a particular form of sheep, the Swaledale, better suited to the conditions. Slightly smaller than lowland sheep, with a distinctive black face and legs, and curved horns, the sheep are sure to be seen along the way.

The first part of the walk from Keld follows the line of the Upper Swaledale corpse road that linked the upper communities with Grinton and the closest piece of consecrated ground. To ease the burden of a journey that could be as long as 25 km (15 miles), the corpses were carried in wicker coffins.

(2) Kisdon Force

Here, as in the southern dales, the underlying rock is from the Yoredale Series and selective erosion has created another series of fine waterfalls. Of these Kisdon Force is the most attractive, the water dropping over ledges of exposed rock in fine style. Interestingly, although the local names are mainly Norse, the name Kisdon is older, dating from the Dales' Celtic era. The

name means 'small hill', the hill in question lying to the south of the falls.

(3) Tan Hill

Leland, the Elizabethan traveller, noted that 'the men of Suadale were much used in digging lead ore'. He was merely noting the continuation of mining that had been going on at least since the time of the Romans. In its medieval, and later, form the mining was by 'hushing'. A mountain stream would be dammed to create a large reservoir. The dam was then broken to create a torrent of water that ripped off the soil and exposed the ore-bearing rock. The scars of such hushes can still be picked out: North Hush, on the western side of upper Gunnerside Gill, is perhaps the best local example. The walk passes close to the old Beldi Hill lead mines, and there are numerous old remains on Stonesdale Moor. The largest concentration of old sites lies to the east, on the moors between Upper Swaledale and Arkengarthdale, an area where the mines employed several thousand people 200 years ago, producing 40,000 tons of lead annually.

On Tan Hill, however, it was not lead but coal that the miners sought. The seams were thin and the coal of poor quality, but it had been worked since the 13th century at least (when the coal was used to heat Richmond Castle) and continued to be worked until the 1930s when the mines finally became uneconomic. Transport was always a problem even after the horse and cart had been replaced, the yield and the coal's quality not meriting the construction of a railway. The shafts passed on the walk are air shafts, dug to change the air in the horizontal mines.

The Tan Hill Inn refreshed the miners. At 528 m (1732 ft) it is the highest in England, which makes it a favourite with motorists, cyclists and walkers. It is an almost legendary

The Tan Hill Inn

landmark for those walking the Pennine Way. When county boundaries were redrawn in 1974 the inn, which had stood on the Yorkshire side of the Yorkshire-Durham border, was moved into Durham: a local outcry caused the planners to think again and quickly restore the inn to its rightful county.

The inn was managed by a series of colourful hosts and hostesses, none more so than Susan Peacock, hostess for thirty-five years until her death in 1935, who is remembered in the rough-cut memorial behind the inn. She was apparently much like the local weather, sunny and amiable or harsh and frosty, depending upon her mood, and was greatly missed when she died.

Tan, the name of the hill, derives from the same root – meaning 'fire' – that gives us Beltane, the Celtic festival when fires were lit on Walpurgis Night. It is likely, therefore, that the hill was a sacred site for communing with the spirits of the dead, a thought which might stir walkers into ensuring that they reach the inn or Keld before nightfall.

(4) Robert's Seat House
Robert's Seat is another Old Norse name, but the house is much later, having been built in the 14th century for 'watchers', men who patrolled the moor looking for poachers.

The North York Moors

The North York Moors are an upland area with well-defined boundaries – the North Sea, the Vales of Pickering and York, and the Tees Valley. Within that upland area are a whole series of small moors (usually taking their names from their defining dales), some 150 of them, delineated by over a hundred dales. The larger dales define areas of uplands which have been given specific names – for instance, the Tabular Hills to the south, and the Hambleton Hills to the west – but despite this appearance of distinct features, the Moors have a single identity, defined by geology and climate. Only on the coastal plain where a layer of fertile glacial moraine overlies the base rock is there a distinct change.

The rocks of the North York Moors were laid down in the Jurassic period of geological time, about 170 million years ago. They are sedimentary, laid down as sand and mud below a sea or river delta. The chief rocks are of the Lias series, fossil-rich rocks: the ammonites that occur in the coastal Liassic rocks gave rise to the legend of St Hilda (of Whitby Abbey) and the snakes, and account for the incorporation of ammonites into the abbey's crest. The Lower Lias rocks, the first to have been laid down, are soft shales. The overlying Middle Lias are sandstones and ironstones, the latter the basis of the now-extinct Cleveland iron industry whose ruins are seen on several of the walks described here. Roseberry Topping, arguably the most distinctive feature of the Moors, owes its shape to ironstone mining. The Upper Lias rocks also include ironstones, and the inclusion within them of alum and jet led to other industries, though only jet extraction has survived the passage of time.

The Lias rocks were overlaid by a further sea beneath which the limestone of the Tabular and Hambleton Hills was laid down. But unlike the limestone of the Yorkshire Dales, the Moors limestone is not water-soluble. The Moors limestone is oolitic, a compact rock formed from small rounded grains (hence the name, from the Greek for 'egg stone'), its water-resistance meaning that there are none of the cave features so common in the Dales.

As with the Yorkshire Dales, the last Ice Age sculpted the Moors, though here the actual process was different. It is believed that there was no permanent ice cap above the moors, the upland block deflecting glaciers around it. These glaciers impaired the natural drainage of the Moors, a situation which became critical when meltwaters began to build up. The channels cut and deepened by these meltwaters imposed the pattern of dales and moors we see today. Another feature of these surrounding glaciers was the morainic deposits left by their retreat. These have created an encircling ring of fertile land, a contrast to the high moors and the wooded dales.

The high moors of the North York Moors are the largest expanse of heather moorland in England, a marvellous sight in July and August when whole areas turn purple. The moors are used for sheep grazing – here, as in the Yorkshire Dales, the main sheep is the Swaledale – but the drystone walls that are such a feature of the Dales are absent. The reason is that the heather – ling, bell heather and cross-leaved heath – is the home of red grouse, the moorland owners of the 19th century being more interested in shooting on the moors than in enclosing them. On several of the walks described here shooting butts – stone-built and topped with heather or bilberry so that the guns blend with the natural surroundings – can be seen. The grouse shooting season lasts from 12 August to 10 December. The arguments about the ethics of the shooting and whether it is responsible for the maintenance of the moorland are too big a subject to be discussed here.

The North York Moors National Park was created in 1952 to protect the uplands and defining dales, an area of 533 square miles. It is a less varied landscape than the Yorkshire Dales, and with fewer distinctive features. But it is also a wilder country and one with a number of enigmatic and evocative historical sites. It is a land for the connoisseur, and forms the second of the two main focuses of walking in this book.

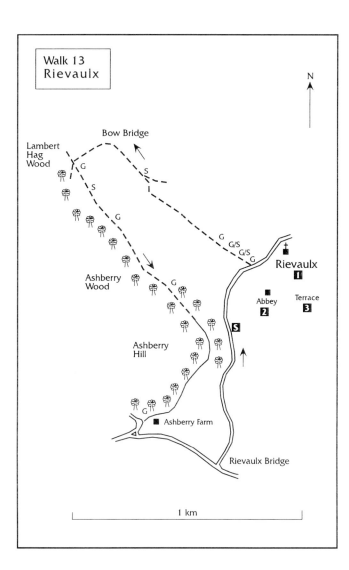

Walk 13
Rievaulx

N

Bow Bridge

Lambert
Hag
Wood

G

S

S

G

G
G/S
G/S
G

Rievaulx
†
1

Ashberry
Wood

G

Abbey
2

Terrace
3

S

Ashberry
Hill

Ashberry Farm

G

Rievaulx Bridge

1 km

Walk 13 Rievaulx

Though not as complete as Fountains, Rievaulx Abbey is, if anything, an even more romantic and picturesque ruin. This short walk enjoys a magnificent view of the abbey as it explores beautiful Ryedale.

Walk category: Easy (1 hour)

Length: 4 km (2.5 miles)

Ascent: 45 m (148 ft)

Maps: Landranger Sheet 100, Outdoor Leisure Sheet 26

Starting and finishing point: At 575849, in the lane south of Rievaulx village, close to the abbey. The abbey car-park is reserved for visitors to the ruin.

From the parking place, head northwards along the lane towards Rievaulx village (see (1) Rievaulx), with the Abbey (see (2) Rievaulx Abbey) and terrace (see (3) Rievaulx Terrace) to your right. Go through the village, soon reaching a signed footpath, on the left, for Bow Bridge. Go through a gate and cross the field beyond to a gate/stile. Cross and follow the fence and trees on the right to reach another gate/stile. The embankments to your right defined the canal that supplied water to the abbey in medieval times.
    Go over the stile, through a gap and over several further stiles to reach a lane, bearing left to reach Bow Bridge, a picturesque packhorse bridge over the River Rye. Beyond the

bridge, head towards Lambert Hag Wood on the hillside ahead to reach a junction of paths: select the one for Ashberry, turning left through a gate. Go over a stile, through a gate and ascend wooded Ashberry Hill. As compensation for the climb – the only ascent on the walk – the views to the abbey are magnificent, though when the walking in the wood is at its best (when the trees are in full leaf) the view can be limited and fleeting.

The path goes around the eastern flank of Ashberry Hill, then descends towards Ashberry Farm, which is passed on your left. Turn left past the farm (which is fronted by a green that would grace a small village), crossing a small bridge and bearing left to reach a road. Turn left and follow the road to reach Rievaulx Bridge over the River Rye. Cross the bridge, taking great care as it is very steep and you are in a blind spot to approaching cars, and turn left just beyond it to return to the start.

(1) Rievaulx

Rievaulx is a marvellously picturesque village where ancestors of Lord Wilson (Sir Harold Wilson, twice the Prime Minister) lived. The church is on the site of the abbey's Gate Chapel where guests removed their travelling boots and changed into slippers. Occasionally such chapels were known as Slipper Chapels, though that does not seem to have been a common name here. In 1906 the remains of the chapel, which had been built in the 13th century, were incorporated into the new village church. The abbey gate actually had inner and outer gatehouses, one housing the chapel, the other the gatekeeper. Remnants of this other gatehouse can still be seen near the entrance to the churchyard.

(2) Rievaulx Abbey

Rievaulx was a Cistercian foundation. The order chose remote sites for their abbeys so that the monks could maintain an

Rievaulx Abbey

independent and harsh existence, the Cistercians having broken away from the Benedictines because they believed that the rules of St Benedict – who had founded that order – had been softened to such an extent that they were no long being correctly observed. The abbey was built on land given by Walter l'Espec of Helmsley as a memorial to his son who had been killed in a riding accident. It was land that fitted the wild site requirements of the Cistercians exactly: there were wolves and wild cats in the tangle of woods and the abbey was so remote that years later a visitor still spoke of the 'vast and dreadful isolation'.

Despite these apparent disadvantages, the abbey – whose curious name (pronounced Reeve-O) derives from its position in Ryedale, Rye Vallis as it would then have been called – became one of the major Cistercian houses in Britain, its holdings extending to over 6000 acres and 15,000 sheep. Much less has survived than at Fountains, the other major Cistercian house in Yorkshire, but what has is marvellously evocative. The church is the largest early Cistercian church to have survived, being even larger than any in France. Its soaring walls and simple, austere design are a powerful symbol of the order's own ideals. It was built during the tenure of the third abbot, St Aelred, a great scholar and a man of equally great piety. Aelred loved Rievaulx, claiming that it offered 'a marvellous freedom from the tumult of the world'. In old age Aelred was crippled by arthritis, a condition aggravated (and possibly originally caused) by the cold and damp of the abbey, a fire only being allowed in the communal warming house and in the infirmary. The monks sought a dispensation from the mother Cistercian house at Citeaux in France for their abbot to be allowed a fire in his lodge. This was readily agreed, but Aelred declined the offer, remaining in his unheated quarters until his death.

Rievaulx Abbey

(3) Rievaulx Terrace

When Rievaulx Abbey was suppressed in 1538 there were just twenty-two monks left, the house having declined considerably from its heights, when it was home to 140 monks and more than 500 lay-brothers. The land and buildings were granted to the Earl of Rutland and through him passed to the three local families of Manners, Villiers and Duncombe. In 1758 Thomas Duncombe had the 800 m terrace laid out above the abbey, building a temple at each end. The temples are in Greek style, one Ionic, the other Doric, and are among the finest surviving examples of Georgian landscaping architecture in Britain. From the terrace visitors could look down on real medieval ruins before retiring to the classically domed and pillared temples for refreshment. The terrace is now a National Trust property and is worth visiting for its views of the abbey and Ryedale alone. The entrance lies to the north of the village, off the road linking the village to the Helmsley road.

Walk 14 The Bride Stones

This short walk visits one of the most unusual features on the North York Moors, a feature reached at the end of a long drive through the Dalby Forest.

Walk category: Easy (1 hour)

Length: 4 km (2.5 miles)

Ascent: 70 m (230 ft)

Maps: Landranger Sheet 94, Outdoor Leisure Sheet 27

Starting and finishing point: At 878905, the Low Staindale car-park. The car-park is reached by the Dalby Forest Drive, a toll road through the vast Dalby Forest. There is a Visitor Centre in Low Dalby, in the beautiful Thornton Dale, which has information on both the forest and the local area.

From the car-park, head north-westwards to reach a gate and map. The gate will be taken by the return route. For the outward route either the steep climb up Jonathan Gill or the shallower climb through Low Wood can be taken. Either route is very well defined. If the steeper route (heading northwards) is followed a left turn is necessary to reach the Low Bride Stones. The route through Low Wood, starting as a track but becoming semi-paved, leads directly to the Low Bride Stones (see (1) The Bride Stones). The view from the outcrops is superb, taking in moorland and forest, and the High Bride

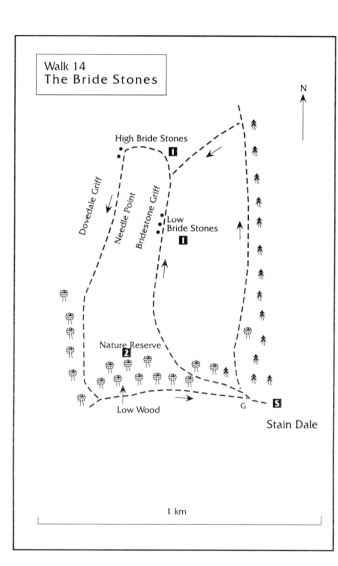

Walk 14
The Bride Stones

N

High Bride Stones

1

Dovedale Griff

Needle Point

Bridestone Griff

Low
Bride Stones

1

Nature Reserve

2

Low Wood

G

S

Stain Dale

1 km

Stones across the incised valley of Bridestones Griff (see (2) Bridestones Nature Reserve).

Now continue northwards along the semi-paved path, dipping down into Bridestones Griff and then rising to reach the High Bride Stones. There, turn sharply left to descend the narrow heather-covered ridge of Needle Point which separates Bridestones Griff from Dovedale Griff. The path is still semi-paved and stepped where necessary. Cross the stream that combines the flow of the two small streams from the Griffs and turn left to follow it southwards (walking with it on your left hand) to reach a footbridge. Use this to recross the stream and then bear left at a cross-tracks to follow the edge of Low Wood, on your left. Go through the gate seen on the outward leg of the walk and reverse that outward leg to return to the car-park.

(1) The Bride Stones

There are several 'bride stones' on the North York Moors, the name being given to stone circles on Bilsdale East Moor, a few kilometres south-west of Whitby, as well as the outcrops here. In the case of the stone circles it is probable that the name derives from ancient fertility rites performed at the circle for newly married women. Such practices are probably pagan in origin, but as 'bride' is an Anglo-Saxon word it seems likely that the practices continued for many centuries after Christianity had been established in Yorkshire. It is certainly the case that such rites were practised in other parts of Britain until just a couple of hundred years ago.

The Bride Stones visited on the walk almost certainly derive their name from the Norse word for 'edge', the stones defining the boundary of the local moorland. The outcrops were shaped by differential erosion of sandstone laid down in the Jurassic Era of geological time. The sandstone – known as the Passage Beds – is composed of silicon- and calcium-based rock. As the calcium-based rock weathers more quickly than the silicon-based rock the sandstone, which was exposed to the elements

(and to the ice of the Ice Age) some 60,000 years ago, has eroded into the curious shapes we now see. The 'top heavy' nature of some of the outcrops derives from differential erosion within the outcrop itself, the base rock being softer than that at the top. Of the two outcrops, the Low and High Bride Stones, the Low are the more impressive, though the views from each are equally good.

The stones here should not be confused with the Wainstones which sit on the Moors' western escarpment above Carlton-in-Cleveland. Those stones, popular with rock climbers, are named from the Saxon word for howling, though it is not clear if that comes from the noise of the wind as it moans between the stones or from the area's use as a burial ground, the howls being the laments of the grieving.

(2) Bridestones Nature Reserve

The 873 acre Bridestones estate was bequeathed to the National Trust in 1944 by Mrs R. F. A. Whitney. Of the bequest about 300 acres form the Nature Reserve, which was created in 1966 to preserve the dwarf shrub heath and the wildlife it supports. The Reserve is an SSSI (Site of Special Scientific Interest) and is managed by the Trust in conjunction with the Yorkshire Wildlife Trust. The Reserve's plants include not only moorland species, such as ling, cross-leaved heather and bilberry, but rarer species such as tormentil and the insectivorous sundew. The woodland is chiefly sessile oak, but there are also birch, ash and other deciduous and conifer species. The insect life includes the rare Emperor moth, while the bird life includes not only the more common moorland species such as wheatear and whinchat, but the rarer hen harrier.

The Low Bride Stones

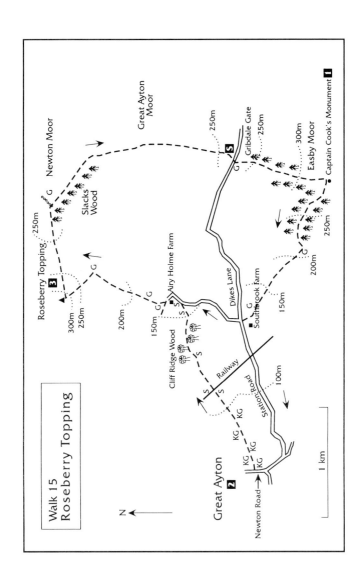

Walk 15
Roseberry Topping

N

Great Ayton **2**

Newton Road

Station Road

1 km

Railway

Cliff Ridge Wood

Airy Holme Farm

Southbrook Farm

Dikes Lane

Roseberry Topping **3**

Cook's Monument **1**

Captain Cook's Monument **1**

Easby Moor

Great Ayton Moor

Newton Moor

Slacks Wood

Gribdale Gate

300m

250m

200m

100m

150m

200m

250m

300m

250m

250m

150m

Walk 15 Roseberry Topping

At the northern tip of the Cleveland Hills, the hills which define the western edge of the North York Moors, lies Roseberry Topping, one of the National Park's most distinctive features. This fine route visits the peak, and also follows a section of the Cleveland Way to the Cook Monument on Easby Moor.

Walk category: Intermediate (3 hours)

Length: 11 km (7 miles)

Ascent: 340 m (1115 ft)

Maps: Landranger Sheet 93, Outdoor Leisure Sheet 26

Starting and finishing point: At 592110, the car-park at Gribdale Gate.

From the car-park, turn right along the road, then left through a gate signed with the distinctive National Trail acorn, the waymarker for the Cleveland Way. Follow the broad track beyond uphill to the Cook Monument (see (1) Captain Cook's Monument). Now turn sharp right (north-westwards) and follow a path between two old gateposts. Continue with an old wall on your left, then bear left to descend into a conifer plantation. Continue to descend, now very steeply, through the plantation, crossing a forest road and then exiting the plantation through a gate into a field. There are fine views of the Cleveland Plain from here.

Cross the field by keeping close to the wall on the right, turning right where the wall ends to continue downhill along a rough track. Go through a gate and descend a tree-lined lane to reach a road (Dikes Lane). A short-cut is now possible, following the lane opposite directly to Airy Holme Farm. The best walk continues by turning left and following the road to a t-junction in Great Ayton (see (2) Great Ayton). Turn right along Newton Road, then, after about 90 m, turn right again through a kissing gate and follow a signed footpath through two further kissing gates and a thicket, passing Cleveland Lodge on the left. Go through further kissing gates, then over a stile on to the Esk Valley Railway. Cross the railway and another stile. Now follow the field edge (with a fence on your left) and go over a stile into Cliff Ridge Wood.

Go steeply uphill through the wood to reach a path junction. Go straight over, continuing steeply uphill, firstly on a zigzag-ging made-up path, through further woodland to reach a stile. Cross and turn right along the field edge to reach another stile. Cross and bear left, heading downhill, now with a fence on your right, to reach another stile (in the fence). Cross, go down steps and turn left along a metalled farm road to reach Airy Holme Farm.

Bear left through the farm, turning right to go through a gate. Follow the track beyond towards Roseberry Topping. Keep ahead where the track bears right, then fork left and climb steeply to the top of the peak (see (3) Roseberry Topping). Turn right at the summit, following the ridge path, then descending steeply to reach an old wall. Climb uphill with the wall on your right, passing a conifer plantation, also on the right, to reach a gate on to Newton Moor. You are now on the Cleveland Way again. Bear right along the Way, with the plantation (Slacks Wood) and the wall on the right, heading southwards and descending to regain the starting car-park.

(1) Captain Cook's Monument

James Cook was born on 27 October 1728 in a two-roomed thatched cottage at Marton, then a village but now a suburb of Middlesbrough. James' father was a farm labourer but was offered a better job at Airy Holme Farm, Great Ayton, moving there when the boy was eight. After leaving school, James was apprenticed to a grocer and haberdasher in Staithes. In that fine port the young man fell in love with the sea and as soon as his apprenticeship was completed he joined a Whitby collier company. He would have achieved his first command in 1755, but as war with France was looming he joined the Royal Navy. Cook was a bright seaman, soon mastering the skills of navigation and surveying which he put to use in 1762 when he surveyed the coast of Newfoundland, a trip that followed soon after his wedding to Elizabeth Batts.

In Newfoundland Cook witnessed a solar eclipse, his account to the Royal Society persuading them to appoint him to the command of *Endeavour*, a Whitby collier that was being sent to Tahiti to watch Venus traverse the sun. The expedition to Tahiti was a success, but while there Cook opened secret orders that led him to even greater discoveries in the southern ocean. In October 1769 Cook sighted North Island, New Zealand (which had been sighted a century earlier by Tasman). Cook's survey of the country discovered that it was two islands (separated by what is now called Cook Strait). Later, in June 1770, while on his way to survey Australia's eastern coast, Cook discovered the Great Barrier Reef by the simple method of ramming his ship into it while (apparently) sailing in 17 fathoms of water. *Endeavour* sustained little damage and returned to Britain in triumph in 1771.

In 1772 Cook returned south, crossing the Antarctic Circle; on this trip he also proved the value of lemon juice in preventing scurvy. In 1776 he left Britain on his final voyage. After exploring the Bering Straits and the coast of Alaska in a search for the Pacific entrance to the North-West Passage, Cook

sailed to Hawaii. There a boat was stolen from his ship, the *Discovery*. Cook arrested the Hawaiian king as a hostage against the boat's return, but in a confrontation on the beach on 14 February 1779 he was stabbed in the back by a native.

Those interested in discovering more about this great sailor can visit the Cook Museum in Whitby, occupying an 18th century merchant's house where Cook is known to have lodged, or the Cook Schoolroom Museum in Great Ayton (see below).

(2) Great Ayton

It was in this large, but attractive, village that the young James Cook lived and went to school. The school, in High Street, now houses a museum to the great man. The cottage where the family lived was dismantled in 1934 and moved to the Fitzroy Gardens in Melbourne. Even the creepers that grew around the cottage were dug up and replanted. This amazing move was not without problems, the last owner of the cottage adding a note to her will that it should not leave Britain when she heard there was interest from America. After much persuasion she substituted 'Empire' for 'Britain'. An obelisk marks the spot where the cottage stood. The village also has a Heritage Trail, a short walk linking local places associated with Cook.

Even without the Cook associations Great Ayton would be an attractive village to visit, its mix of old stone and new houses lining the banks of the River Leven. There are two churches, the older of which, All Saints, has remnants from earlier, both Saxon and Norman, buildings.

(3) Roseberry Topping

The peak is an outlier of the Cleveland Hills, separated by the erosional effects of wind, rain and frost, only a sandstone cap saving it from complete destruction. Its name is Norse, a

Captain Cook's Monument on Easby Moor

corruption of Odinsburg, after Odin, the supreme god of the Viking pantheon, the god of creation, victory and death. The second part of the name is also Norse, from *toppen* – peak.

Early drawings of the peak show it to have been almost perfectly conical, its present irregular, but distinctive, shape being the result of extensive quarrying in the late 19th century. Beneath the sandstone there was ironstone, and men toiled to remove the ore to local smelters. Unfortunately, by 1912 the quarrying had so undermined the cap on its northern side that it partially collapsed into the workings. No one was injured, but the lesson does not seem to have been learned, and further undermining was carried on until, thankfully, the quarry become uneconomic and ceased in 1929. It is likely that the cap's collapse was aided by the action of the spring that saw the legendary death of Prince Oswy (see Walk 20 – Osmotherley). In medieval times the spring was believed to have healing powers, particularly for eye problems. The locals also used the peak as a barometer, a couplet noting that 'If Roseberry Topping wears a cap, Cleveland must beware a clap.'

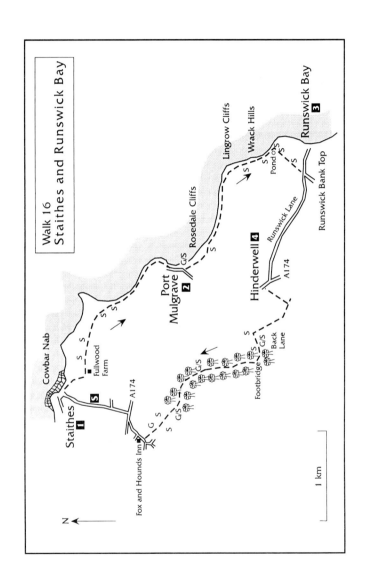

Walk 16
Staithes and Runswick Bay

Cowbar Nab

Staithes **1**

S

A174

Fox and Hounds Inn

Fullwood Farm

S

S

S

Port Mulgrave **2**
G/S

Rosedale Cliffs

S

Lingrow Cliffs

Wack Hills

S

S

Pond S

S

Runswick Bay **3**

Runswick Lane

Hinderwell **4**

A174

Runswick Bank Top

S

G/S

Back Lane

Footbridge

G/S

S

N

1 km

Walk 16 Staithes and Runswick Bay

The Cleveland Way is a fine route, crossing high moor and following rugged coast to produce a National Trail of excellent contrasts. Of the coastal sections of the route, one of the best links Staithes, one of Britain's most picturesque small ports, set in a tight inlet, to Runswick Bay, equally pretty, but positioned in the almost perfect semicircle of water that shares its name.

Walk category: Intermediate (3 hours)

Length: 11 km (7 miles)

Ascent: 80 m (260 ft)

Maps: Landranger Sheet 100, Outdoor Leisure Sheet 26

Starting and finishing point: At 781186, the car-park in Staithes. In summer this car-park fills rapidly and it may be easier to start the walk in Runswick Bay, where there is a car-park at 808161.

From the car-park, go down Staithes Lane to the harbour (see (1) Staithes). Go past the Cod and Lobster Inn and turn right up Church Street, passing Captain Cook's Cottage. Go up the steps at the end of the street and turn left (there is a sign for the Cleveland Way) to follow a narrow, steep path to the cliff top. From here the Cleveland Way is very clear: cross fields linked by stiles with marvellous views ahead towards Kettle Ness and back towards Staithes. The route is one field away from the cliff at first, but soon reaches it: at this point the view back includes a sight of the cliffs at Boulby which, at 207 m (679 ft) are the tallest in England.

Continue along the cliff top to reach Rosedale Lane which is followed into Port Mulgrave (see (2) Port Mulgrave). Opposite No. 79, go left (as signed for the Cleveland Way) to regain the cliff path. The route now follows a delightful section of coast, at first above Rosedale Cliffs, then, after going around High Lingrow, Lingrow Cliffs and Wrack Hills. Caution is needed if there are children in your party as there are occasional sections without a cliffside fence and the cliffs, with their little water-falls, and an exciting sea at their base, are very inviting.

Now look out for a stile on the right by two ponds. This is usually well signed, but there have been occasions when the sign has been removed. If you miss the turn do not panic: the cliff path also reaches Runswick Bay, though in a less straight-forward manner. Go over the stile and past the ponds – notable for their irises and reeds and, judging by the signs, for their newts. Follow the path across fields and stiles to reach the Runswick Bay Hotel on Runswick Bank Top. To visit the village (see (3) Runswick Bay), and to reach the alternative start, turn left. The village is well worth a visit, but it lies at the bottom of a very steep hill.

Our route turns right, leaving the Cleveland Way and following Runswick Lane to Hinderwell (see (4) Hinderwell). The lane joins the A174 in Hinderwell: turn right along the main road for about 60 m. Now cross, with great care, and turn left between Ivy Cottage and Jasmine Cottage. This is a public right of way despite the suggestion that you are only allowed to go as far as the surgery. Continue through the houses and school, crossing a field to reach Back Lane. Turn right and follow the lane to its end. There, turn left over the stile, cross the field beyond and go over another stile. Now follow the footpath over a further stile and into Borrowby Dale. Cross a footbridge over the dale's beck, go up steps and turn right to follow a hedge back into the wood. Bear left just inside the wood, bearing left again at the next path junction. Leave the wood at a gate/stile and follow a path over two stiles to reach a footbridge. Cross and follow the track beyond to reach a lane. Turn right, passing the Fox and Hounds Inn, and following the road to reach the A174 again. Turn right, then cross the main road – again with great care – to turn left into Staithes. Follow the road through the upper village to return to the car-park.

(1) Staithes

The bridge over Staithes Beck is one of the most photographed spots in this most photographed of villages. The normal backdrop for such shots is Cowbar Nab, a cliff of loose rock. A rock fall from this cliff once decapitated a young Staithes girl whose ghost is said to haunt the bridge. The Nab is also responsible for the fact that the port's houses are so tightly grouped together and are facing north, exposed to winter's fierce and cold winds. Small wonder that James Cook, who was apprenticed to a haberdasher in the town, become such a hardy sailor. The shop in which Cook served has long since disappeared into the sea, despite the naming of Captain Cook's Cottage. The plaque on the cottage, unveiled by the Prince of Wales in 1978, notes Cook's eighteen months in the employ of William Sanderson, but is careful not to imply that the cottage is authentic.

The loss of land and houses at Staithes – in reality the port is only half the village, a more modern half standing on the hill above the older section – is due to the easily eroded boulder clay on which the port stands, though a local legend suggests a more romantic reason. The story is that two mermaids were washed ashore in a huge storm, and were found exhausted on the beach. Rather than freeing them when they had regained their strength, the village folk held them captive for many months, making money by charging visitors to see them. When the mermaids eventually escaped they swam a little way out

to sea then turned and cursed the village, saying that the sea would eventually flow to Jackdaw's Well. And so it has.

There are still a few boats – known as cobles – left of the fishing fleet that was once the mainstay of Staithes. In those days the menfolk would catch herring in summer and cod during the rest of the year while their wives knitted guernsey jumpers against the cold. Today the catch is salmon and lobster. Interestingly the old inn beside the sea, the Cod and Lobster, embraces the old and new catches in its name. It is said that the bowsprit of a boat once broke one of the inn's windows, so close does it sit to the sea.

Leaving Staithes, the walker might like to contemplate an event held during a festival and sports day in Staithes in 1797. The event, the biggest of the day, was advertised as: 'a fish skin purse containing SILVER will be run or rolled for in sacks, a man and a boy in each sack'. Both the event and the prize are intriguing.

(2) Port Mulgrave

There is little now to see of the old port here, built in the 19th century to export iron ore extracted from local mines. Cowbar Nab at Staithes is, in part, ironstone and was quarried at one time. The ore was transported from the mines to the port by a narrow-gauge railway which tunnelled its way directly to the sea so as to avoid negotiating the cliff. Port Mulgrave was never economic and eventually fell victim to the coastal erosion which plagues this section of the coast, though the name lives on in the village passed on the walk.

(3) Runswick Bay

The port here has the advantage over Staithes of being sheltered from northerly winds by Lingrow Knowle. It has, however, suffered the same problems with coastal erosion. In 1682

Cowbar Nab, Staithes

the village was almost entirely lost when the land slid into the sea. Then, in 1829 the village at the far end of the bay was completely lost when a vast area of Kettle Ness disappeared under the waves after days of torrential rain. On that occasion considerable loss of life was avoided only because a ship was fortuitously anchored off-shore and took on the villagers.

(4) Hinderwell

This village, once noisy with miners and mining traffic, is now a quiet little place, reflecting its origins as a retreat for the Whitby abbess St Hilda who came here to escape the pressures of monastic life. St Hilda's Well, which gave the village its name, can still be seen in the churchyard. It was blessed by the saint and for many years its waters were claimed to have healing powers.

Runswick Bay

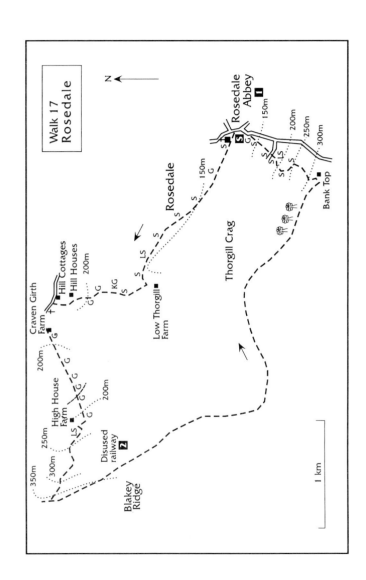

Walk 17
Rosedale

N

Rosedale Abbey

Rosedale

Thorgill Crag

Bank Top

150m
200m
250m
300m

Craven Girth Farm

Hill Cottages
Hill Houses

200m

Low Thorgill Farm

High House Farm

Disused railway

Blakey Ridge

200m
250m
300m
350m
200m

150m

1 km

Walk 17 Rosedale

Rosedale is one of the quietest valleys of the North York Moors, a peaceful, secluded place seemingly at one with the ruins of the abbey that named its major village. It comes as a surprise to discover that in the last century the valley was full of the bustle of one of the most important iron ore mines in northern England.

Walk category: Difficult (3 hours)

Length: 12 km (7.5 miles)

Ascent: 300 m (980 ft)

Maps: Landranger Sheet 94, Outdoor Leisure Sheet 26

Starting and finishing point: At 725960, either of the two car-parks in Rosedale Abbey.

From either car-park, go across the village green and turn right along the lane to the church (see (1) Rosedale Abbey), passing it to reach two signed footpaths. The route follows the further one: go over a stile and bear right through a caravan site to reach another footpath sign. Bear right again, go through a gate and follow the field edge close to the caravan site, to reach a stile. Go over this and another further on into a small wood. Do not cross the footbridge on the left: instead, continue to a path fork, taking the left branch there to follow the stream. Cross another stile and follow waymarkers across fields to reach a ladder stile. Cross the field beyond to reach another stile. Go over and bear left along a track, following it down to reach a footbridge to the north of Low Thorgill Farm.

Again you do not cross the footbridge: instead, bear right, away from it, heading northwards along a path to reach a stile in the middle of nowhere (!) and another in a hedge. Cross the field beyond to a kissing gate, and the field beyond that to reach a gate. Go through and bear left to reach a gate. Go through and along a semi-enclosed path to reach Hill Cottages – a terrace of old ironworkers' cottages – going around to their left to reach a road.

Turn left, following the road past the old Ebenezer Methodist Church and a guest house. Just beyond, turn left along a farm lane (signed as a footpath). Go through a gate into the farmyard of Craven Girth Farm. Now maintain direction through the farmyard, going through another gate and continuing along the edge of the field beyond (with a fence on your right) to reach another gate. There are old mine workings to your right here.

Go through the gate and again walk with a fence, and then hedges, on your right to reach another gate. Go through, walk downhill beside a stream, crossing another field and bearing left to reach a gate. Cross the farm track beyond to the gate opposite, go through and walk with a fence on your right to reach another gate. Go through and bear left to reach a ladder stile a little way past another gate. Cross the stile and walk to a waymarker post. Turn left, as indicated, and go uphill, sometimes along a clear, but winding, path, sometimes across pathless ground, but always heading for the ridge top.

At the ridge you will join a wide track, the trackbed of the old iron-ore railway (see (2) Rosedale Railway). Turn left along the track. This is not a public right of way, but is a permissive path: please obey the Country Code as the owners of the land have specified that adherence to the Code is necessary for its continued use. From the track there is a fine view of Rosedale.

Eventually the track reaches an unfenced road which can be followed (turn left) back to Rosedale Abbey. A more satisfactory route leaves the track just before it reaches a house some 400 m short of the road. Walk towards the house, turning left down a wide grass track about 90 m before reaching it. Follow the track downhill, then take a narrow path on the left – the main track continues to reach the road – to reach a stile. Cross and descend steeply to reach a stile over a wall. Go over this and another stile on the right a little further on. Now follow a path across a golf course, bearing left in front of the sheds and going over a stile on to a lane. Cross to the stile opposite and follow the right edge of the field beyond to an awkward stile. Go over and descend steps beside a house to reach a gate. Go through on to a road (the road from the end of the old railway track) and continue ahead to reach a t-junction. Turn left to return to Rosedale Abbey.

(1) Rosedale Abbey
In 1158 William of Rosedale founded an abbey for Cistercian nuns in this peaceful valley. The abbey was never successful, falling prey several times to raiding Scots, most particularly in 1322 when it was virtually demolished. Although partially rebuilt it did not regain its former size. When the abbey was dissolved in 1536, what little remained was used as a handy quarry by the locals, many of the valley houses being constructed of abbey stone. As a result, apart from the parish church of the village of Rosedale Abbey, which incorporates parts of the old abbey church, almost nothing now remains of the abbey buildings.

Rosedale, in which the village sits, is a beautiful valley, alive with daffodils in springtime. It is less hospitable in winter: when William the Conqueror crossed the local moor while beating the boundaries of his new realm he was caught in a storm so violent that the moor was named Blackmore, a name still used until the middle of the last century.

(2) Rosedale Railway

Although ironstone had been mined and smelted locally for centuries – the monks of Byland Abbey operated an iron smelter even when Rosedale Abbey was occupied – it was not until the 19th century that the ore was mined on any scale. The early commercial production was not encouraging for share-holders, the company returns for 1860 noting simply 'Much raised, not any sold.' But things did improve. At first horse-drawn carts hauled the ore to Whitby, but the size of the operation and the new furnaces at Middlesbrough soon required a different mode of transport. A railway was therefore laid from the Rosedale mines to the top of the scarp slope at Ingleby Greenhow. The moorland track was a meandering one, it being cheaper to lay track than to build bridges, and it is that track that our walk follows. It was at the Ingleby end that the railway was most impressive however. There a 1 in 5 incline took loaded ore trucks downhill, the loaded trucks hauling empty trucks up the slope. This operation involved a single haul wire and a drumbrake. On one occasion the heat gener-ated by braking set fire to the drumhouse, burning it to the ground and stopping use of the incline for some time. Worse still occurred if the wire parted – which it did – when the fully laden trucks would hurtle down the incline scattering men in all directions.

The railway opened in 1861 and along it 10 million tons of ore were hauled before it finally closed in 1929. By the last years the railway was hauling less in a year than it had in a week at the height of mining operations. The population of Rosedale Abbey declined in parallel. In 1850 there were about 500 inhabitants; by 1870 this had risen to almost 3000, but had declined to below 300 a hundred years later.

Ruin beside the old Rosedale railway

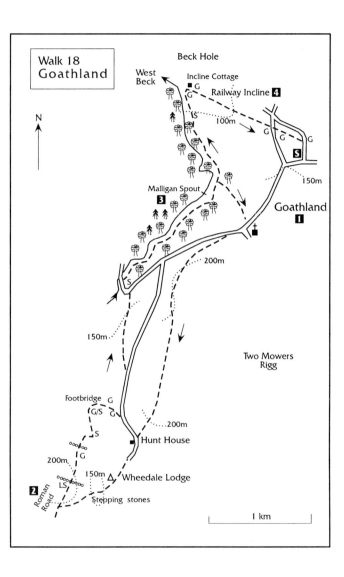

Walk 18
Goathland

Beck Hole

West Beck

Incline Cottage
G
G
Railway Incline **4**

N

S
100m
G
G
G

S

150m

Malligan Spout
3

Goathland
1

200m

S

150m

Two Mowers
Rigg

Footbridge G
G/S
G

S

200m
G

200m

Hunt House

LS
150m △ Wheedale Lodge
2
Roman Road
Stepping stones

1 km

Walk 18 Goathland

As a centre for visitors to the North York Moors National Park Goathland has an enviable list of attractions. It is reached by a steam-hauled railway, and another railway trackbed of considerable historical interest is nearby. It is close to a fine section of Roman road and scenically it is superb, the high moors come almost to the doors of the houses, and the wooded valley of the West Beck – complete with an impressive, but picturesque, waterfall – is quite lovely. As if more was required, the coast at Whitby is only a few miles away. This walk visits all the local scenic and historical highlights.

Walk category: Intermediate (3.5 hours)

Length: 13 km (8 miles)

Ascent: 270 m (885 ft)

Maps: Landranger Sheet 94, Outdoor Leisure Sheet 27

Starting and finishing point: At 834013, the car-park in Goathland.

From the car-park, turn right to reach the main village road and turn right along it, bearing left to follow it gently uphill to reach the church (see (1) Goathland). Just beyond the church there is a road junction: continue ahead for about 100 m, then bear half-left along a clear, grassy path that heads across the open moor. The path curves gently leftwards and upwards, staying parallel to the road, then climbing more steeply towards a shallow moorland ridge. The views from the ridge, in all directions but especially to the west (right), are magnificent. The rocky outcrops here are a favourite haunt of adders, though the walker will need to be lucky (rather than unlucky) or quiet and patient to see one. As you advance along the ridge the path becomes less well defined, but the descent to Hunt House (at 815987) is straightforward. When the metalled road is reached, turn left and follow it to its end, continuing along the stony track to the youth hostel at Wheeldale Lodge.

Go to the left of the Lodge, following a clear path that descends steps to Wheeldale Beck. Here the walker crosses the line of the Lyke Wake Walk. Cross the beck using the excellent stepping stones and go steeply uphill, at first on steps, then up a difficult sandy path; the sand is home to thousands of mining bees. At the top of this steep climb is the Roman road (see (2) Roman Road). Turn right and follow the road to reach a ladder stile. Cross and continue along the road to a gate in a wall. Here the road ends, the wall itself probably being the further remains of the road. Go through the gate and follow the wall on the right to reach a stile. Cross and descend to a gate and stile. Go through and bear right, ignoring a footbridge and ford to the left, to reach another footbridge a little further on. Cross and turn right, following a broad track to reach a road near Gill View.

Turn left and follow the road for about 500 m to reach a signed footpath on the left. Take this, following it downhill then bearing right along a fence to reach another road. Though there is a footpath sign here there is no stile over the fence. Turn left and follow the road steeply downhill, bearing right with it to reach a bridge over West Beck. Just before the bridge, go right, over a stile, and follow the path beyond beside the beck. The next 2 km (1.25 miles) of the walk are through wonderful country, but the path is rocky and frequently slippery because of the tree cover, and requires caution if a fall, or even a slip into the beck, is to be avoided.

After about 1.5 km (1 mile) the Mallyan Spout waterfall (see (3) Mallyan Spout) is reached. Continue along the path, soon reaching a path on the right that offers a short-cut back to Goathland (follow the path to a road and turn left). Go over a footbridge and climb the path beyond to a stile. Go over and follow the left edge of several fields, linked by stiles, to reach a gate by Incline Cottage. Go through the gate and turn right to reach another gate. Beyond this is the incline of an old railway (see (4) Whitby to Pickering Railway). The incline offers a gentle climb, at first along a rough, tree-lined track, to a road. Cross the road and continue along the old trackbed, now a pleasant grass track. When another road is reached, turn right, soon reaching the starting car-park.

(1) Goathland

This scattered village, the houses loosely grouped around a large green, is another fine centre for visiting the North York Moors. It has been such a centre since the coming of the railway, as the number of good hotels shows. The village church, dedicated to St Mary, was built in the 1890s by the architect W.H. Brierley. With its stone roof and unusual low, oblong tower between the chancel and the nave, it is a delightful building. Inside, the stone altar and font are believed to be 12th century, perhaps from the first church on the site. The church may stand on the site of a hermitage church, also to St Mary, built in the twelfth century: in 1117 Henry I granted land at 'Godeland' to Osmund, a priest, so that he could pray for the soul of Queen Matilda.

The origin of the village's name is unclear, the only certainty being that it is not named for goats. From the documented original it is conjectured that it may be Norse for Goda's Place, or it might be from God's Land, perhaps taking the name after the hermitage church had been built.

(2) Roman Road

The road across Wheeldale Moor is one of the best-preserved sections of Roman road in Britain. It is seen at its best on this walk. The road was built in about AD 80 and is 5 m (16 ft) wide, made with flat stones laid on gravel, with kerbstones, culverts and side gutters for drainage. It is believed that the road linked the town of Malton to the coast, perhaps serving the signal station near Kettleness or the military camp at Whitby. The precise route of the road is debatable as it is clear for only an 8 km (5 miles) section. It is only known with certainty that it passed the legion camp at Cawthorn.

The road is known as Wade's Causeway after a local giant. Wade is said to have built the road between his castles at Pickering and Mulgrave (each of which, of course, he built single-handed). Wade is also said to have created the Hole of Horcum when he scooped up a handful of earth to throw at a rival. Blakey Topping is said to have been created when the earth, missing his rival, landed.

(3) Mallyan Spout

This superb waterfall is over 20 m (about 70 ft) high. Be cautious if you are tempted to take a close look, the boulders at the base of the fell are very slippery.

(4) Whitby to Pickering Railway

The railway line from Whitby to Pickering was designed and engineered by George Stephenson and opened in 1836 with horse-drawn trains. There are disputes about which of the world's railways was the first to carry fare-paying passengers, but all agree that this was one of the first three or four. Stephenson's route was brilliantly conceived, utilizing a deep, narrow gorge in Newton Dale – cut by glacial meltwaters at the end of the last Ice Age – to enter the Vale of Pickering and

The Roman road above Goathland

tunnelling through the Moors near Grosmont. On the final section to Pickering trees, sheep fleeces and cowhides were laid across a bog to carry the track. The real problem lay at Goathland however. Here the track had to climb 60 m (197 ft), the last stage of the haul up on to the moor. To overcome the problem Stephenson built the incline from Beck Hole. The incline, at 1 in 15, was too steep for horses and so a rope hauling system was installed. A water tank was filled at the top of the incline, the descent of the filled tank (which weighed 4 tons) hauling coaches up. At the bottom the water would be released, descending coaches hauling the empty tank back up. The ascent took about five minutes. This system worked, but was dangerous, the rope snapping on several occasions. To increase security, the rope was replaced by a wire hawser, but even after a steam engine had been installed to do the hauling the system was still prone to failure. On one memorable occasion the wire hawser parted sending a trainload of herrings crashing to the bottom of the incline. Legend has it that the stench of rotting fish filled Goathland for weeks. After several more near misses it was decided to abandon the incline in favour of blasting a shallower route up to the village. Ironically, the decision to create the new track was taken just before the most serious accident – in February 1864 – when the hawser broke and several coaches went careering down the incline. Two passengers were killed and thirteen others were injured. The newly carved route was opened on 1 July 1865.

Although passengers did use the line, it was mostly used for freight, a fact that eventually led to its closure by British Rail in 1965 after a serious decline in freight traffic. For many railways closed at the same time the fall into disrepair was swift and irreversible, but here a Preservation Society was formed in 1967 and the line reopened in 1973. Today both steam and diesel engine draw trains for the benefit of visitors and locals, while the old incline offers a splendid walk.

Walk 19 Westerdale Moor

Westerdale is one of the most remote parts of the North York Moors, offering a walking environment for the connoisseur. This route follows a section of the Lyke Wake Walk and visits several of the ancient crosses for which the Moors are famous.

Walk category: Difficult (4 hours)

Length: 14 km (8.75 miles) or 17 km (10.5 miles)

Ascent: 350 m (1150 ft)

Maps: Landranger Sheet 94, Outdoor Leisure Sheet 26

Starting and finishing point: At 665057, in the village of Westerdale. Parking is also available, with care, beside the unfenced moorland roads roughly half-way around the route, and at the moorland car-park at 682999.

From the centre of Westerdale (see (1) Westerdale), go down the lane beside the village church (the church is on your left). Follow the road past a marvellous old shooting lodge (formerly a youth hostel, but now privately owned), on your right, and Hall Farm. The road is now little more than a metalled strip: continue along it, going through two gates, the second at its end. Beyond that final gate, go left along the track towards New House Farm. The track curves gently right, then goes more sharply right and downhill for about 90 m before rising to the farm. There, go left through a gate on to a signed footpath, following the path across two fields and over a

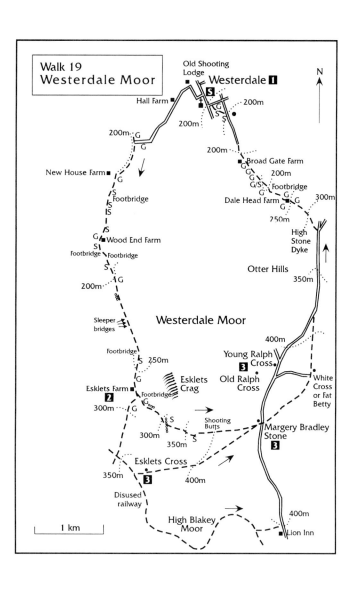

Walk 19
Westerdale Moor

Old Shooting
Lodge

Westerdale 🔳1

Hall Farm

S

200m

200m

G

200m

Broad Gate Farm

200m

G

G

200m

New House Farm

G

200m

G/S

Footbridge

S

Footbridge

G

G

300m

Dale Head Farm

IS

250m

S

G/

Wood End Farm

High
Stone
Dyke

S

Footbridge

Footbridge

Otter Hills

S

350m

G

200m

Westerdale Moor

Sleeper
bridges

400m

Footbridge

S

250m

Young Ralph 🔳3
Cross

G

Esklets
Crag

Old Ralph
Cross

Esklets Farm 🔳2

Footbridge

White
Cross
or Fat
Betty

G

300m

G

S

300m

350m

Shooting
Butts

S

Margery Bradley
Stone
🔳3

350m

Esklets Cross

🔳3

400m

Disused
railway

High Blakey
Moor

400m

Lion Inn

N

1 km

footbridge. Continue with the River Esk on your left, crossing fields linked by stiles to reach a farm road. Cross this and another stile, and head towards Wood End Farm.

Bear right through a gate and go behind the farm to reach another gate. Go through and walk with farm buildings on your left to reach a stile. Cross this and the footbridge ahead, then follow the Esk to reach another footbridge, on your left. Cross the bridge (or the ford beside it) and turn right along the footpath signposted for Farndale. The footpath stays close to the Esk, on your right, as it leaves the beautiful Westerdale scenery, heading upwards towards the bleaker, but no less attractive, moorland of Westerdale Moor. Go through several fields linked by gates and stiles, then cross open country to reach a footbridge (at 656022).

Cross the footbridge and continue, with the river now on your left, to reach a stile. Cross this and two fields beyond to reach the ruins of Esklets Farm (see (2) Esklets Farm). There is a new building to the left here. At this point there is a choice of routes. The shorter one follows the route of the Lyke Wake Walk which crosses the open moor to the east of Esklets. Just beyond Esklets, after crossing the stream and where the clear track bears right, turn left and descend to a footbridge. A faint but obvious path, with occasional white arrows, now ascends beside an old wall. When the path disappears, head for the obvious break in the wall above in which there is a stile. Cross and follow a now clear path to a stile over a fence. Beyond, the path is occasionally difficult to see: follow the line of shooting butts to reach a good track. As the moorland road is approached, the longer route joins from the right. The road is reached close to the Margery Bradley Stone, at 674014 (see (3) Moorland Crosses).

The Lyke Wake route is a permissive rather than a public path, the right of way, and an alternative section of the Lyke Wake Walk, following the clear track to a gate. Beyond, bear left across open moor to reach a remote footpath sign, at

654007. Bear left there, going along the trackbed of the old Rosedale Railway (see Note 2 to Walk 17). Another shorter alternative route soon presents itself, bearing left off the trackbed to reach Esklets Cross (see (3) Moorland Crosses) from where a rough track heads east and north-east to reach the Margery Bradley Stone.

The longer route follows the trackbed for about 3 km (just under 2 miles), to reach a signed path on the left. Take this, going uphill to reach the road near Blakey Howe and the Lion Inn. Turn left and follow the road to the Margery Bradley Stone.

From the stone there are also two alternative routes. The shorter of these heads north-east along the signed bridleway that threads its way through the heather. There are superb views into Rosedale, to the right, on this section of the walk. Follow the path as it swings northward to reach a road and White Cross (see (3) Moorland Crosses).

The alternative route follows the road northwards to reach a junction with a minor road branching off right. To the left here are two further crosses, the Old and Young Ralph Crosses (see (3) Moorland Crosses). Turn right along the minor road to reach White Cross.

From White Cross, continue northwards along the signed bridleway, following a series of marker stones to reach a road. Continue ahead, still northwards, along the road to reach a road junction, with a minor road branching off right. At this junction turn half-left along a signed bridleway, passing High Stone Dyke – a poorly understood feature, possibly dating from medieval times – to your left. Follow the path down to Dale Head Farm. Go through a gate and turn left to go between the buildings. Bear right and walk past the farmhouse. Go through the right-hand of a pair of gates and cross two fields, keeping to the wall on your left. Cross a footbridge over Tower

Young Ralph Cross

Beck, go through a gate and cross the field beyond to another gate. Now cross two further fields, linked by a gate, to reach Broad Gate Farm. Go through the farm buildings and continue along the farm lane. Just before reaching a crossroads, a signed path on the left crosses fields to cut off the corner made by the lanes.Turn left, then turn right to return to Westerdale.

(1) Westerdale
This delightful little village, grouped around its sturdy 19th century church, is one of the most remote on the North York Moors. In medieval time this remoteness attracted the Knights Templar to Westerdale. This order of religious knights was founded in 1118 with the aim of protecting pilgrims to the Holy Land from bandits, but eventually raised preceptories – as their religious houses were called – throughout Europe. Although noble in their aims the Knights became rich and powerful and the order was suppressed in 1312 when Europe's rulers become fearful of it. Nothing now remains of the Westerdale preceptory.

The solitude that attracted the attentions of the Templars attracted a different group when there was a youth hostel in Westerdale Lodge, built in Victorian times for gentlemen shooting grouse on the heather moors and now a private house. Much older is the packhorse bridge known as Hunter's Sty. It probably dates from medieval times, but has been restored since then. Perhaps Awd Mally used the bridge at night while out searching for milk to steal. Awd Mally was a local witch-hare, that is a witch who could turn herself into a hare, the better to explore the area. The North York Moors abounds with tales of such hares being shot – it was necessary to use silver bullets to inflict damage – only for an old woman in the village to be discovered the following day with identical wounds to those suffered by the hare. Awd Mally seems to have been too sly for the farmer who hunted her as a hare, turning on him and frightening him out of his wits.

(2) Esklets Farm

It is believed that the farm was the first inhabited site in Westerdale. That first building was erected as a shepherd's lodge on land given to Rievaulx Abbey by the Norman Lord de Brus. The shepherds who tended the flocks were lay-brothers from the abbey, armed to protect the sheep from wolves.

(3) Moorland Crosses

Westerdale Moor has a number of interesting old crosses, all probably erected as either boundary markers or waymarkers for travellers on this loneliest of moors. Esklets Cross marks the boundary of the Farndale and Westerdale parishes. White Cross, with its broad stump and Celtic-like cross, is also known as Fat Betty. One of the Ralph Crosses is very old, as is its name, the charter of Guisborough Priory for the year 1200 mentioning 'Crucom Radulphi'. It is not clear whether the reference is to Old or Young Ralph Cross, though the names doubtless give a clue. Young Ralph Cross is one of the best of the Moors' crosses, though the present version – almost 3 m (9 ft) high – is an 18th century replacement of an earlier one. The top of the cross is hollow, an old custom requiring rich travellers to leave a coin for the benefit of poor pilgrims. The placing of the coin from a horse would present no problems, but retrieving it if you were walking would be a trickier task. The custom continues to this day, and was almost the undoing of the cross in 1961 when someone attempting to retrieve a coin snapped the slender column. The repair was a real act of craftsmanship, but further repair was necessary in 1984 when vandals draped a rope over the cross and used a car to haul it down. Young Ralph is the emblem of the North York Moors National Park.

One story of how the crosses received the name Ralph relates how an 18th century traveller died of exhaustion at this point on the moor during a winter crossing. A local farmer called

Ralph, touched by the man's tragic death, erected the stone as a memorial. Perhaps this legend, which seems to have little basis in fact, arose when the original cross was replaced at around that time.

Another story links Ralph's Cross, Fat Betty and the Margery Bradley Stone. Sister Elizabeth, a nun at Rosedale Abbey, and Sister Margery from Baysdale Abbey agreed to meet on Westerdale Moor, about half-way between the abbeys. Sister Elizabeth brought with her Ralph, an old man who helped out at the abbey. It was a filthy day, with thick fog settled over the moor top. Ralph started to look for Sister Margery, but failed to find either her or Sister Elizabeth again. The three sat alone until the fog lifted to reveal that they were just yards apart. Ralph erected the stones as a permanent reminder of the day.

In the 17th century, the Margery Bradley Stone, occasionally called simply the Margery Stone, more in keeping with the name of a nun, was an assembly point for the distribution of alms to the poor.

Fat Betty

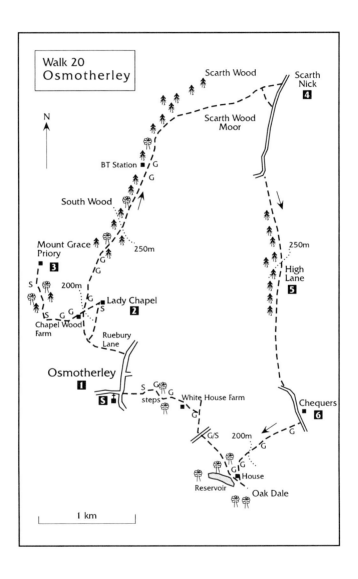

Walk 20
Osmotherley

N

Scarth Wood

Scarth
Nick
4

Scarth Wood Moor

BT Station ■ / G

G

South Wood

Mount Grace
Priory
■ 3

250m

High
Lane
5

S

200m

G

G

S G G
Chapel Wood
Farm

■ Lady Chapel
2

S

Ruebury
Lane

Osmotherley
1

S

S
steps

G

G

G

White House Farm

G

Chequers
■ 6

G/S

200m

G

G

G

G

Reservoir

■ House

Oak Dale

1 km

Walk 20 Osmotherley

Set high on the Cleveland scarp at the eastern edge of the North York Moors, Osmotherley is a delightful mix of old and new buildings. From the village, which overlooks the Vale of Mowbray, the Cleveland Way – one of Britain's National Trails, official long-distance footpaths – heads north towards Mount Grace Priory and on to Scarth Nick. From there an old drove road is used to regain the Cleveland Way south of the village.

Walk category: Intermediate (3.5 hours)

Length: 14 km (8.75 miles)

Ascent: 280 m (920 ft)

Maps: Landranger Sheets 93, 99 and 100, Outdoor Leisure Sheet 26

Starting and finishing point: Osmotherley church. There is an alternative start at 469993 on the road to Scarth Nick and Swainby.

From the church in Osmotherley (see (1) Osmotherley) go north along the road signed for Swainby, following it uphill out of the village. Ignore the first footpath to the left (Grant Close), continuing to reach Ruebury Lane, also on the left, which is signposted for the Cleveland Way, and follow it around Ruebury Hill. The lane forks near a memorial: the Cleveland Way goes ahead to Chapel Wood Farm, but we bear right on a path signed for the Lady Chapel (see (2) Lady Chapel).

Walk past the chapel, following the wood edge on the right to reach a stile on the left. Cross this and turn left, downhill, to reach Chapel Wood Farm. From the farm a worthwhile 3 km (about 2 miles) detour can be followed to Mount Grace Priory: go through the farmyard, bear left through a gate and follow a path to another gate. Follow the path beyond with a hedge/ fence on your left. Go over a stile into a plantation and bear right, downhill, to reach a stile. Go over and cross a field to reach the car-park of the priory (see (3) Mount Grace Priory). Return along the same route to Chapel Wood Farm.

Now follow the Cleveland Way northwards, bearing right at a path fork to walk through South Wood. Continue along the wood edge, following it to the British Telecom Microwave Radio Station. The station is passed by a clear manoeuvre over low stiles and through gates, crossing the access road. Beyond, there are excellent views to both left and right. The path bears right through two walls (gates and/or stiles): fork right beyond the second to cross Scarth Wood Moor. The track leads to the road at Scarth Nick – a V-shaped notch carved in the moorland edge by glacial meltwater at the end of the last Ice Age – close to the start of the Lyke Wake Walk (see (4) Lyke Wake Walk), but a short-cut to the road turns sharp right along a track reached about 100 m after joining a wall on the left.

Turn right along the road, soon reaching a point where it turns sharp right near an unofficial car-park (the alternative start). There, go straight on, crossing a footbridge and following the broad track beyond uphill (see (5) Hambleton Drove Road). Follow the old drove to reach a road. Turn left along the road to Chequers (see (6) Chequers). Continue along the road for about 50 m, then turn right along a wide, signed track. The path follows the wall on the left, losing height steadily to reach a house in Oak Dale. Turn sharp right around the house to reach the first of the dale's two reservoirs. You are now back on the Cleveland Way. Follow the Way past the reservoir and uphill to reach a road. Turn left for about 50 m, then go right

along Green Lane (signed for the Cleveland Way). Bear left to
follow the lane past White House Farm, keeping the buildings
on your left. The waymarking here is good, though there is
little evidence of a path for the next few metres. Go downhill
to cross another lane and, soon after, reach a footbridge over
Cod Beck. This is a beautiful spot, known locally as Happy
Valley. Cross the bridge and go steeply up steps to reach a
squeeze stile into a field. Cross a field to another squeezer into
an enclosed path. Follow the path to Back Lane, Osmotherley,
continuing along a cobbled path past St Anne's Cottage and
the Methodist Chapel to emerge under an archway into the
main square at Osmotherley.

(1) Osmotherley
The Saxon King Oswald had a son, Oswy, whose death was
foretold by a seer. The boy would drown on a particular day
the seer said. Oswy's mother took him to Roseberry Topping
on that day, a peak both remote and dry. It was a hot day and
she lay down to rest, wearied by her fears. When she woke she
found Oswy lying face down in a previously unknown spring.
She brought the dead prince to this village, then called Teviot-
dale, where he was buried. But as he was being lowered into
the ground Oswy's mother died of grief. The two were therefore buried together. The villagers, overcome by the sadness of
the occasion, changed the name of the village to recall that 'Os-
by-his-mother-lay'.

   It is an interesting legend, but one poorly supported by hard
evidence, only a cross shaft and tombstone in the churchyard
suggest any settlement before the Normans arrived. For centuries after, raids by the Scots made life hard for the villagers: one
raid in 1315 was so devastating that Osmotherley was exempt
from taxes for four years. Only in the 18th century, when alum
was discovered in Oak Dale and Cod Beck was used to drive
linen mills, did the village achieve any prosperity. At around
the same time John Wesley preached in the village. The

villagers were eager converts to Methodism, the village's
Methodist Chapel (erected in 1754) being one of the earliest in
Britain, and Wesley returned many times. His last visit was in
1784 when he was eighty-one. For his early sermons Wesley
used the curious stone slab set on four uprights that stands
beside the old village cross. This had been a barter table where
market produce was sold and, in addition to the preacher, also
supported coffins being carried from outlying farms. The
coffins would rest here while the bearers regained their breath
for the last steps to the church.

(2) Lady Chapel

The name is a short form, but experts are divided as to whether
this was Our Lady's Chapel or Lady Catherine's Chapel. The
evidence for the first is that this was a chapel of ease for Mount
Grace Priory which was dedicated to the Virgin Mary, while
that for the second is the curious legend of Thomas Parkinson
of Thirsk. Parkinson's first son was stillborn and buried in a
shallow grave which was opened by crows. Seeing this appal-
ling act as a sign from God, Thomas and his wife gave up their
possessions, she becoming a nun and he a hermit. Catherine of
Aragon is said to have given money for Thomas to build a
hermitage chapel – hence the name, and also the name of one
of Osmotherley's inns, the Queen Catherine. When Mount
Grace Priory was dissolved, Parkinson was evicted and wan-
dered the country aimlessly. He married, bigamously, in Bridg-
north, then became a hermit again in Stow-on-the-Wold, but
was 'unmasked' and imprisoned.

At Mount Grace's dissolution, the Lady Chapel escaped
destruction and soon became a pilgrimage centre for local
Catholics. This may have been because it was the only complete
Catholic church locally, but many have suggested another
reason, one also based on local legend. One version of this says

The village cross and old barter table, Osmotherley

that the remains of St Cuthbert were brought here from Durham at the start of Henry VIII's purge, while another says that the body of Margaret Clitherow, the wife of a York butcher, who was executed in 1586 for sheltering priests, is buried here.

(3) Mount Grace Priory

Mount Grace was not begun until 1398, very late in the monastic history of England, and was for the Carthusian order, not one of the major orders of English monks. The Carthusians had been founded in 1184 to return to a more solitary form of monasticism, each monk having his own cell and maintaining a hermit-like existence, the charterhouse (as Carthusian settlements were called) existing merely for reasons of security and economy. This solitary life – which only the truly committed favoured – lead to the Carthusians opposing Henry VIII's reforms vigorously: of the nine charterhouses in England, the priors (heads) of three were executed, as were several monks. Prior John Wilson of Mount Grace survived and took a pension when the priory was dissolved in December 1539.

The monks' cells at Mount Grace were on two floors, the ground floor having a living room with a fire, a bedroom and study. No second floor has survived, but it is likely that these were workshops: Carthusian priories were the publishing houses of their day, the monks copying books and manuscripts. Each monk also had his own garden for growing herbs and vegetables. There was a communal dining-room for meals on special days, and the monks congregated in the small church for services. But the solitary existence was maintained to such an extent that the cells' serving hatches were angled so that the monk did not see the person bringing his meal.

(4) Lyke Wake Walk

The Walk takes its name from the Lyke Wake Dirge, an ancient dialect poem dating from at least the 15th century and probably earlier. The poem's name is, in turn, derived from *lyke*, corpse – which also gives us lych in lych-gate – and refers to the time when corpses were carried across the moor for burial at one of the few plots of consecrated ground. The journey along these defined moorland corpse roads was believed to be reversed by the souls of the dead. The souls had to endure tests at places like the Bridge of Dread before making their way to Paradise. The Walk was devised in the 1950s by Bill Cowley of Swainby, walkers who successfully complete its 40 mile crossing of the moor in 24 hours becoming dirgers and being awarded a coffin badge. However, the Walk became so popular with charity and challenge walkers that the route became a horrendous quag-mire-like track. Consequently the National Park authorities began to discourage walkers. Today the walk is unofficial and crossings by large groups are discouraged, but it is still a fine test piece, though the difficulties of early dirgers (when navigation was added to stamina as a necessary requirement for completion) have virtually disappeared.

(5) Hambleton Drove Road

In the days before refrigeration, cattle, pigs and sheep were brought to market live, drovers escorting the animals along defined drove roads. Inns were set up along the roads for the use of the drovers, who were rich on their return journeys and, therefore, very popular with landlords. The rich drovers were also popular with highwaymen who lay in wait on quieter sections of the roads. In the case of the Hambleton road it is likely that the drovers were following in the footsteps of Bronze Age folk – and certainly in those of the Romans – who also used this route to cross the western moor.

Oak Dale

(6) Chequers

This ancient drove inn became ruinous after the drovers departed, but has been restored as a working farm, small camp site and worthwhile refreshment point for walkers on the Cleveland Way (and this walk). The old inn sign has been restored and once again declares, 'Be not in haste. Step in and taste, Ale tomorrow, For nothing.' The sign disappeared in 1960 but was thankfully found in 1984 at Northallerton.

Walk 21 Lilla Howe and Falling Foss

One of the features of the Moors, particularly the eastern section, is the number of old crosses that can be found in surprisingly remote places. It is believed that these were set up by the monks of the Moors' many monastic houses to mark tracks across the wilder sections of moorland. This route visits several such crosses, including one of the most famous, and a very picturesque waterfall.

   Note: This route crosses a remote part of the moor where the walking can be difficult, especially after prolonged wet weather.

Walk category: Difficult (4 hours)

Length: 16 km (10 miles)

Ascent: 180 m (590 ft)

Maps: Landranger Sheet 94, Outdoor Leisure Sheet 27

Starting and finishing point: At 889035, the car-park at the Falling Foss waterfall, reached from the B1416 which heads south from Whitby to link with the A171.

Take the path that leaves the far end of the car-park, heading south-west towards the May Beck car-park. According to the information board in the car-park this path is waymarked, though these marks are far from obvious. However, the path is clear enough, passing through beautiful mixed deciduous woodland (with numerous nestboxes in the trees) to reach the

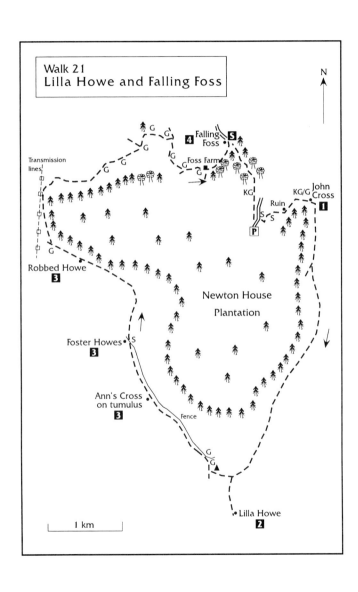

Walk 21
Lilla Howe and Falling Foss

N

Transmission lines

G
G
G
G
G

Falling Foss **4** S

Foss Farm
G
G

KG

KG/G John Cross **1**

Ruin
S S

P

Robbed Howe **3**

G

Newton House Plantation

Foster Howes **3** S

Ann's Cross on tumulus **3**

Fence

G
G

Lilla Howe **2**

1 km

May Beck car-park. The car-park is the other side of the beck: do not cross, continuing to reach the access road.

Turn left for 50 m or so, then turn right along a signed footpath that rises steeply through dense bracken. Go over a stile and walk past a ruin to reach another. The footpath now bears left and then back right rather than following the forest edge on the right, to reach a kissing gate which gives access to the open moor. Just beyond the gate is the stone shaft of John Cross (see (1) John Cross). Do not turn right at the cross: instead, follow the track ahead for 60 m to reach a signpost and turn right along a path that runs southwards through the heather, walking parallel to the forest edge and passing several waymarking posts (Nos 7, 8 and 9).

At Waymarker No. 9, do not take the path ahead (marked 'Trail'): instead, bear left on a rough path marked by mountain bike tracks climbing gently through the heather. The heather and bog make the path indistinct sometimes, but maintaining a course parallel to the forest edge will keep you roughly on the route of the old Robin Hood's Bay Road. Losing the route is problematic as the heather is knee-deep and difficult to traverse, so please take care. If you do lose the path, turn right and head for the forest edge – which should never be more than 200 m away. If you do not regain the path by doing this then you had strayed to its right rather than its left and you will need to head back out from the forest edge to regain it.

Eventually, as the path rises, it becomes less prone to being lost in bogs and easier to follow: continue along it (there is a convenient solitary conifer tree, which looks at first like a cairn, to act as a waymarker – unless it has been felled) to reach its junction with a broad crossing track. There is a signpost here, but the real waymarker is the cross on Lilla Howe just a couple of hundred metres away. A visit to the cross (see (2) Lilla Howe) is a detour from the route, but is an absolute must.

Return to the cross-tracks and turn westwards (signed Goathland), soon passing the trig. point summit of Stony Leas to reach another track junction near an old cylindrical trig. pillar. Turn right, go through a gate and bear left away from the next gate along a clear, broad track. The walk is now sandwiched between MoD land, to the left, and forestry land, to the right. The consequences of straying from the track could be dire!

Follow the track to reach Ann's Cross on Tumulus – on the left, at 878001 – (see (3) Ann's Cross on Tumulus), continuing along the track to reach a gate at Foster Howes. Go through and follow the track as it bears left along Whinstone Ridge, a perfectly straight intrusion of basalt that runs from Esk Dale to Fylingdales Moor. The track moves closer to the forest edge on the right, heading for the transmission lines ahead. Go through a gate and follow the fence on the right, going with it when it turns sharply right. At the next fence corner, close to a transmission tower and old boundary stone on the left, go ahead, crossing a small stream and bearing right through the heather on a path which becomes more distinct. Follow the path as it runs parallel to the surprisingly deep valley on the right, to reach a gate. Go through and bear left to reach a pair of gates by an old railway truck. Go through the right-hand gate and follow the wall (and then fence) on the left to reach a clearer bridleway bearing right, downhill to Leas Head Farm. At a fence corner, go right, through a gate and follow a track that curves leftwards towards the farm. Before reaching the farm, turn right off the track on a path that soon reaches a sign for Falling Foss. Cross a footbridge, go through a gate and follow the right field edge up towards the buildings marked as Foss Farm on the OS maps. Go through two gates to pass the buildings (on your left), ignoring a path off to the right in favour of the broad track which continues downhill ahead. The track enters the forest: continue downhill to reach an old bridge. To the left here a path runs along the beckside to a footbridge, crossing it to reach a viewpoint for the Falling Foss waterfall (see (4) Falling Foss). From the waterfall the path continues uphill to reach the track which crosses the old bridge. At the top of the rise, turn right to regain the car-park.

(1) John Cross
Only the base of this cross is original, the original shaft and cross head having probably been destroyed by the Puritans. The present, much-shortened, shaft is thought to date from the 18th century and was a boundary marker for the Cholmley Estate, hence the 'C' engraved on the south face. It is speculated that the name derives from a 13th century abbot of Whitby Abbey.

(2) Lilla Howe
Edwin, the Angle King of Northumbria in the early 7th century, was a pagan but married Ethelburga, a Christian princess from Saxon Kent. Ethelburga tried to convert her husband but did not succeed. However, in AD 626 the Queen and her first-born son survived a difficult labour against all odds. Edwin was affected by this, but even more so by his survival of an assassination attempt. His survival was due to Lilla, one of his ministers, who threw himself between the King and the assassin's knife and was killed as a result. Edwin was converted to Christianity and allowed his new son to be baptized. He refused baptism for himself however, claiming that before agreeing to that he wanted his new God to grant him a victory. He won his victory, becoming King of all of England apart from his father-in-law's kingdom of Kent. As a result, Edwin was baptised on Easter Day, 627 in the first, and very recently and hastily erected, York Minster.

Lilla, who had saved the King's life at the expense of his own, was buried with great ceremony in the Bronze Age burial mound below the cross. A quantity of gold and silver, with some rings, ornaments and a brooch, were interred with Lilla's body by a grateful Edwin. The cross stands on an ancient trackway across the moor that delights in the name of Old Wife's Trod.

From the cross the most obvious feature of the moor is the truncated pyramid of the early warning radar station on Fylingdales Moor. The pyramid replaces the golf ball 'radomes' that once dominated the view. Interestingly, it is still the case that neither the old domes, nor the new pyramid, nor the buildings of the station, are marked on the OS maps. Presumably HM Government still believe that any power invading Britain will be completely thrown by this and will be at a loss as to where the station is.

(3) Ann's Cross on Tumulus

This is another ancient cross marking the crossroads of two ancient moorland tracks. Beyond it the walk passes Foster Howes and Robbed Howe. 'Howe' is the local word for a Bronze Age burial mound – as at Lilla Howe. The origins of the names associated with both the crosses – John and Ann's – and the howes – Foster and Greenland's (which lies to the north of the route at 869035) – are lost in time. Only Lilla was important enough for his tale to come down to us. Robbed Howe is more curious. In many parts of Britain, folklore maintained that these (then misunderstood) mounds had been raised over treasure troves. Does Robbed Howe preserve a memory of an early, and successful, search for buried treasure?

(4) Falling Foss

This superb waterfall, dropping into a dark pool, is the best of the falls on the Moors, an area noted for its few, but exquisite waterfalls. The falls has been created by a stream eroding the soft alum shales that lie below the hard 'Dogger' sandstone – the ironstone rock – of the northern Moors. An interesting feature of the falls, and one which distinguishes it from the falls of the Yorkshire Dales, is that an overhanging lip of rock is never created, the Dogger sandstone being formed in large

The cross on Lilla Howe

blocks which crash into the pool whenever a lip is created. The beautiful wooded setting makes Falling Foss justifiably popular with visitors.

The water from the falls flows into Little Beck, a stream that also names a hamlet just 2.5 km (1.5 miles) below the falls. A pool on Little Beck is called the Devil's Dump after a local man, John Reeves, drowned himself there in 1679, filled with remorse after having betrayed an eighty-two year old Catholic priest, Nicholas Postgate, who was executed. Little Beck is also the scene of one of the most enchanting of North York Moors traditions when, in a ceremony each August, a young local girl is crowned Rose Queen and then floated along the beck on a raft.

Walk 22 Whitby to Ravenscar

This second section of the coastal part of the Cleveland Way starts at a town with Dracula connections, passes a picturesque port – Robin Hood's Bay – and ends at Ravenscar, one of the most geologically interesting parts of the Yorkshire coast . Unfortunately there is no direct transport from Ravenscar back to Whitby. For those without two cars, there are numerous buses from Scarborough to Middlesbrough and these call at the Flask Inn (at 931007) about 7 km to the west of Ravenscar (reached by following the Lyke Wake Walk across Howdale and Stony Marl Moors), and also at Robin Hood's Bay. The walk can therefore be shortened by stopping at Robin Hood's Bay, lengthened by a couple of miles by viewing the Ravenscar cliffs and returning to Bay Town or lengthened by walking to the Flask Inn. A longer alternative is to continue along the Cleveland Way to Cloughton (a further 11 km – 6 miles).

Walk category: Difficult (5 hours)

Length: 20 km (11 miles)

Ascent: 280 m (920 ft)

Maps: Landranger Sheet 94, Outdoor Leisure Sheet 27

Starting point: At 899110, the centre of Whitby.

Finishing point: At 980016, the National Trust Centre, Ravenscar.

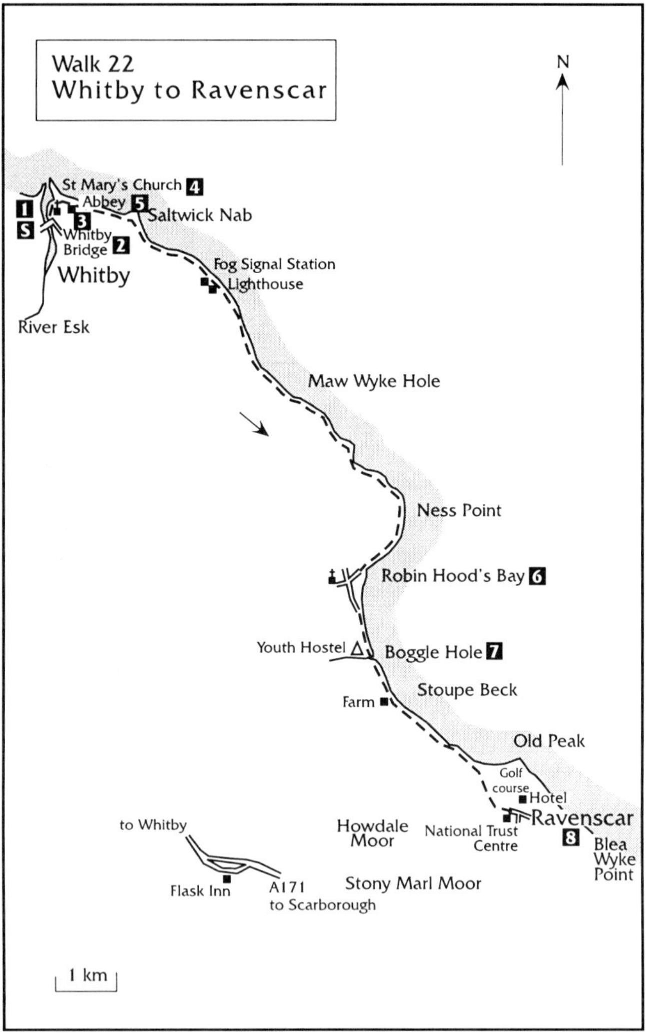

Walk 22
Whitby to Ravenscar

N

St Mary's Church **4**
Abbey **5**
1 Saltwick Nab
S **3**
Whitby **2**
Bridge
Whitby
Fog Signal Station
Lighthouse

River Esk

Maw Wyke Hole

Ness Point

Robin Hood's Bay **6**

Youth Hostel △ Boggle Hole **7**

Stoupe Beck
Farm

Old Peak

Golf
course
Hotel
Ravenscar
to Whitby
Howdale National Trust **8**
Moor Centre Blea
Wyke
Point
Flask Inn A171
to Scarborough Stony Marl Moor

1 km

From the centre of Whitby on Whitby West Side (see (1) Whitby West Side) cross the bridge (see (2) Whitby Bridge) to Whitby East Side (see (3) Whitby East Side). Turn left along Sandgate to the Market Place, bearing right there and then left along Church Street. Bear right to reach the bottom of the 199 Church Stairs, climbing them to reach Abbey Plain (see (4) St Mary's Church and (5) Whitby Abbey). From the abbey, follow the well-signed Cleveland Way which heads east to reach the cliff top and then follows it closely before cutting inland of Saltwick Nab to reach a holiday site. As with the stiles crossed to reach the site, the Way is clearly marked here, the cliff top being quickly regained. Continue along the cliff path, crossing further stiles to reach T'awd Bull, as Whitby's foghorn is known. The horn is deafening and certainly to be avoided if there is fog about.

Continue past the lighthouse to reach a very remote section of coast. Access to the cliffs between the lighthouse and Robin Hood's Bay involves a long walk – the one you are on in fact – and so the walker usually shares the cliff top with a few like-minded souls, the fulmars and gulls. The lucky walker may see common terns or, in winter, turnstones and eider ducks.

The Cleveland Way hugs the cliff edge all the way to Ness Point where the coast turns south and then south-west to reveal the port of Robin Hood's Bay set on the sheltered northern end of the shallow bay of the name. Descend into the town (see (6) Robin Hood's Bay), making your way through the maze of ginnels (alleys) – or via the main street – and then ascending steep steps to regain the cliff. The Cleveland Way now descends to Boggle Hole (see (7) Boggle Hole). Continue as signed, crossing the footbridge over Stoupe Beck before climbing up again to follow the cliff top above High Scar. Ahead now is Ravenscar, a fascinating section of cliff (see (8) Ravenscar). The Geological Trail that explores the cliff follows a steep path up to the Raven Hall Hotel from Peak Steel, the southern pincer enclosing Robin Hood's Bay. That route can be followed if the beach is walked from Stoupe Beck, but care is needed with the tides as escape up the cliffs is dangerous in most places. The Cleveland Way follows an easier route, making a rising traverse above the cliffs before turning inland to skirt the woodland and golf course at Ravenscar. Follow the Way as it circles back towards the coast to reach the National Trust Centre.

(1) Whitby West Side

The early history of Whitby is tied to that of the abbey on the east side of the River Esk. The expansion on the west side of the river resulted from the town's success as a port, initially as a base for a fishing fleet, but later with an expanding trade based on different cargoes. On the North Terrace, high above the point where the sea coast and the River Esk's western bank meet, there is a statue of Captain Cook and a pair of jawbones from a whale. Those two monuments symbolise the history of Whitby's prosperity in the 18th and 19th centuries. Cook used Whitby colliers on his first southern journey. Those tough little boats were manned by equally tough men and carried not only coal but other cargoes from the port. The jawbones are from a huge whale, perhaps 24 m (80 ft) long and weighing 100 tons. It was caught by the Whitby whaling fleet which, from small beginnings in 1753, grew to be the biggest on the North Sea coast. It was a harsh life for the whalers, but even worse for the whales: by 1859 the trade was over, the Arctic whale population so depleted that it was no longer economic to search for them.

Whitby's other notable trade was in jet, the semi-precious black mineral extracted from the local cliffs. Jet was formed from trees that grew 200 million years ago by the same process that has created coal, and it has been used for jewellery since Bronze Age times at least. The Romans powdered jet into wine to cure toothache while in medieval times ground jet in water was supposed to be an antidote for adder bites. Only when

Queen Victoria chose to wear jet as part of her mourning dress for Prince Albert did it become the funereal gem for which it is now mostly known.

Equally funereal is Whitby's association with *Dracula*, Bram Stoker's famous book about the vampire Count. In the book a Russian schooner, the *Demeter*, is driven into the harbour in an oddly sudden storm. All the crew apart from the captain have vanished: the captain is dead. A huge black dog, Dracula in disguise, jumps ashore from the boat and disappears. Dracula spends time in the grave of a suicide in Whitby churchyard before being shipped to London in a crate of earth, a shipment organized by a lawyer living at No 7 The Crescent, a road now known as East Crescent.

(2) Whitby Bridge
The first bridge across the River Esk at Whitby is mentioned in 1351, but the most famous one spanned the river from 1766 to 1835. It was a spindly affair whose moving central drawbridges often became entangled in the rigging of ships passing beneath it. The present swing bridge dates from 1935.

(3) Whitby East Side
The village on the eastern side of the Esk is a marvellous place with a collection of ancient nooks and crannies each with its own history: there are almost 200 listed buildings in and just off Church Street alone. Captain Cook lived in Grape Lane when he was learning his trade as a seaman. The lifeboat near Fish Pier is the latest in a proud line of such vessels. In 1881 when huge seas prevented its launch at Whitby, men and horses hauled the lifeboat 10 km (6 miles) through blizzards – the men's wives holding lanterns – so that it could be launched from a more sheltered spot. Even then many oars were splintered as the boat was pushed out into the freezing waves – but all the crew of the ship in distress were rescued. A less happy event occurred in 1861 when twelve of the thirteen crew of the

lifeboat died within sight of the shore when the boat capsized as it tried to reach a schooner in distress.

(4) St Mary's Church

The 199 Church Stairs existed as early as 1370, the stone steps replacing wooden ones in 1774. The broad steps were constructed so that coffin bearers could rest their load on the way to St Mary's Church. The church was one of which Sir Nikolaus Pevsner was 'fondest of in all England', a stunning tribute owing a little, no doubt, to the fact that St Mary's largely escaped the attentions of Victorian 'restorers'. Though built in the 12th century it was remodelled in the 17th; the work was carried out by shipwrights, a fact which explains why the interior looks like the 'between decks' area of a period battleship. Inside, look out for the Huntrodd memorial to a remarkable married couple. The two were born on the same day, 19 September 1600, and died within five hours of each other on that same date (i.e. 19 September) eighty years and twelve children later.

In the churchyard, Caedmon's Cross is a memorial to England's first hymn writer. Caedmon was a Northumberland oxherd who, though unable to read or write, composed beautiful songs. He became a monk at Whitby Abbey and died there.

(5) Whitby Abbey

In 655, in thanks for his victory over the pagan King Penda of Mercia, King Oswy of Northumberland founded twelve abbeys, one of which was Whitby. The house had both monks and nuns and its first head was the abbess St Hilda. Soon after its founding Whitby Abbey was the scene of one of the most important – arguably *the* most important – events in the history of the English Church. Although nominally to decide upon the

method of fixing the date of Easter, the synod of 664 was actually held to decide whether the Roman or Celtic arm of Christianity would take precedence. The Roman Church was chosen, and ever since there has been a debate on what would have been the outcome for Britain had the decision gone the other way.

Sadly, 200 years after the synod Danish raiders looted the abbey, destroying it completely. For a further 200 years the site lay empty, but in 1078 the abbey was refounded as a Benedictine house. It was a difficult spot for the monks, the site perpetually battered by North Sea weather and raided several times by Norsemen: when it was dissolved in December 1539 it was the poorest Benedictine house in England. Legend has it that when the bells were loaded into a ship bound for London, it sank for no reason in perfect weather while still in sight of the abbey. It is said that the bells can still be heard occasionally, tolling from beneath the sea.

After the Dissolution the roof was stripped and the elements, with free access to the interior, set about demolishing the rest. In this task the weather was aided by two German battleships and a cruiser in December 1914 (375 years and 2 days after the Dissolution), which shelled the abbey during an attack on Whitby. Yet despite these traumas, what remains today is marvellously evocative and the east window, with its triple tier of lancet windows, is still a breathtaking sight.

(6) Robin Hood's Bay
Legend has it that Robin Hood retired here when he became tired of life in Sherwood Forest. There is a Robin Hood's Stone near Whitby said to have been placed where a particularly impressive arrow shot by Robin landed, and two Bronze Age burial mounds close to Bay Town, known as Robin Hood's Butts, are claimed to be where he practised his archery. But

Robin Hood's Bay

none of these stories has any basis in fact (though that is not to say they are not true, just that they are unsupported), and experts claim the name is more likely to derive from Robin Goodfellow, the forest sprite, or from the Norse word *ravn* – raven – which also accounts for Ravenscar to the south.

The town, usually just called Bay Town by the inhabitants, is a pretty place, as picturesque as Staithes but more pleasantly situated. As you walk through it look out for the small upstairs window in each cottage. These are coffin-windows, the stairs being too steep and narrow for a coffin to reach the street other than by being lowered from the window. It is also said that there are secret passages between the houses so that contraband could be passed from the quay to the cliff edge without ever going outdoors.

(7) Boggle Hole

The hole is named for the boggle or goblin, a helpful sprite, said to live here. Off-shore in the bay over 500 species of marine life have been identified to date, including seaweeds, shellfish and sea urchins. The shore is also well known for its fossils, laid down beneath a calm sea in the Jurassic era some 170 million years ago. The easiest to spot are the ammonites. Legend has it that the builders of the first abbey at Whitby were plagued by adders. St Hilda cursed the snakes which all wriggled over the cliffs and were petrified on the shore. These stone snakes – the ammonites – can be seen all the way from Whitby to Robin Hood's Bay. Keen fossil hunters may also find crinoids, gryphaea and belemnites – and even parts of plesiosaurs and ichthyosaurs.

Robin Hood's Bay from Boggle Hole

(8) Ravenscar

Ravenscar was the site of a Roman signal station, but is more famous for its unique geology. Below the Raven Hall Hotel lies the Peak Fault, a distinct fault line in the rocks dating from the Tertiary Era, some 35 million years ago. The fault lies through a series of layers of Liassic rock and it is in these rocks that the bay's fossils are found. The Upper Lias also contains alum which was quarried in the 17th-19th centuries for use in the curing of leather and the making of cloth dyes.

The Yorkshire Wolds

After the land that is now the North York Moors had been laid
down in the Jurassic period, it was first lifted and then
submerged again. Under the next sea, during the Cretaceous
period of geological time, a layer of chalk was laid down.
Chalk is an extremely fine-grained form of limestone, created
from the solidification of the remains of coccoliths (minute
calcareous algae) together with ground shells from other sea
creatures. It is a soft rock, easily weathered when exposed, and
most of the Yorkshire deposits have been eroded away. The
only remaining section forms the Yorkshire Wolds.

The chalk of the Wolds is a continuation of a chalk belt that
extends from southern England, forming the famed white cliffs
at Dover (and the less famous, but more spectacular, cliffs in
Dorset), the North and South Downs and the downland of
Wiltshire. It forms the Chilterns, but then vanishes, reappear-
ing to form the Lincolnshire Wolds. In Yorkshire the chalk ends
in spectacular style at Flamborough Head where its softness
enables the sea to sculpt caves, stacks and blow-holes, to the
delight of the cliff path walker and nesting seabirds.

Chalk absorbs water, quickly forming a sticky mud that is
not to the delight of the walker. But chalk also drains well and
creates one of the most fertile soils in the country. The good
drainage means that many streams run close to the surface,
sometimes above, sometimes below. This peculiar feature of
chalk downland has produced its own naming, the streams
being termed 'bournes' in southern England, and 'races' here
in Yorkshire. In both areas the drilling of artesian wells has
reduced the number of such streams.

In ancient times the Wolds supported agrarian communities,

but the downlands are so good at growing grass that sheep rearing soon dominated. That change was almost certainly a contributing factor to the abandonment of such villages at Wharram Percy (visited on walk 23), though Black Death, too, is likely to have been an important factor. Millington Pastures, visited on walk 24, was a sheep common until as recently as the 1960s when it was enclosed amid a public outcry. Elsewhere, sheep gradually gave way to cereal growing in the 18th century, the change meaning that today much of the Wolds is given over to cereal production. This has had its drawbacks, modern machinery being at its most efficient in huge fields, so that hedgerows have been grubbed out with a consequent loss of wildlife habitat.

The arable nature of Wolds farming means that access to the countryside is more limited than in the Dales and on the Moors and Pennines, routes having to be crafted with care. The two routes described here make the most of this access to visit sites of historical interest in areas of outstanding beauty.

Walk 23 Wharram Percy

This short walk follows a delightful section of the Wolds Way and visits the evocative ruins of a deserted medieval village.

Walk category: Easy (1.5 hours)

Length: 4.5 kms (2.75 miles)

Ascent: 90 m (295 ft)

Maps: Landranger Sheet 101, Pathfinder Sheet 656

Starting and finishing point: At 867645, the car-park for the Wharram Percy medieval village. The car-park lies beside the road that heads west from the B1248 about 0.5 mile south of Wharram le Street.

From the car-park go back to the road and turn right along it, following the Wolds Way. The road climbs gently then descends to reach a sharp right-left dog-leg. Go around the first (right-hand) bend, but then leave the road before the left-hand bend, going straight ahead along a track (i.e. staying with the Wolds Way).

 Follow the Way as it ascends a shallow hill, then drops to the corner of the woodland of North Plantation. Here the Wolds Way continues ahead (south-westwards), but we turn sharp right along a path that drops gently into Deep Dale, a peaceful and extremely attractive narrow valley. Follow the path northwards to enter the Wharram Percy site over a stile. Beyond the stile there is a very attractive pond, to the left, and

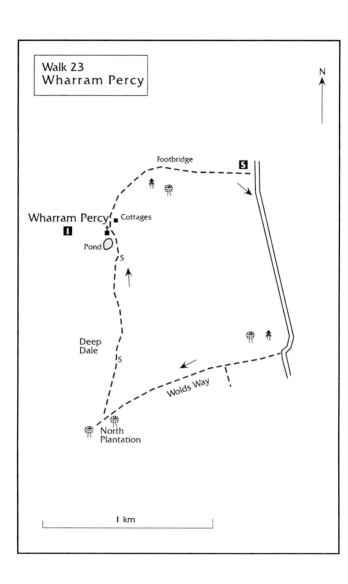

Walk 23
Wharram Percy

N

Footbridge

S

Wharram Percy

1

Cottages

Pond

S

Deep
Dale

S

Wolds Way

North
Plantation

1 km

the ruin of the village church to the right. Aim for the church, surrounding which are the semi-excavated remains of the village houses.

To return to the car-park, head towards the reconstructed cottages that house the Village Research Project. On the left side of these cottages is the sign for the old Wharram railway station which closed in 1950. Now follow the clear path to a footbridge. Cross the bridge and the field beyond to reach an enclosed path that rises steeply back to the car-park.

(1) Wharram Percy

The site in Deep Dale is an ancient one, excavations having revealed the existence of an Iron Age settlement dating from the 1st century BC, and of a Roman villa. The name is Norse, from *hwerhamm*, meaning 'at the bend', an apt description of the village's position in Deep Dale, though the chief excavated remains are of a Saxon village which was probably settled from the 7th century AD onwards – a time of resettlement identified by some scholars as coinciding with the change from paganism to Christianity of Saxon England. The addition to the village's name notes that in Norman times the village was part of the Percy lordship. There were about thirty houses in the village, suggesting a population of 100–150. By 1500 everyone had gone, leaving the village to decay. There was probably no one reason for the exodus, a combination of Black Death, which decimated many local villages, and the change in agriculture from crop growing to sheep rearing being the main explanation. Today all that remains are the mounds of earth on the western side of the valley that mark the position of the houses, the romantic ruins of the church and the cemetery.

The village is in the care of English Heritage, but access is free and allowed at any reasonable time.

Walk 24 Millington Dale

The finest section of the Wolds Way passes through Millington Dale. So good is the walking here that both the North Wolds Walk and the Minster Way also take the dale. Unfortunately it is difficult to organize a circular walk that thoroughly explores the dale but does not involve some road walking. However, the roads are usually quiet and the tarmac-bashing is more than compensated for by the exquisite countryside.

Walk category: Intermediate (3.5 hours)

Length: 12 km (7.5 miles)

Ascent: 270 m (885 ft)

Maps: Landranger Sheet 106, Pathfinder Sheet 666

Starting and finishing point: At 830519, the church in Millington.

From the church, go south-eastwards, downhill, bearing right to reach the Gate Inn. Go past the inn to reach Lilac Cottage, turning left there to descend to Millington Beck. Cross the beck and continue along the road, bearing sharp right just beyond Beck Cottage and climbing steadily up the side of the dale. Bear left with the road to reach Rose Cottages. Continue beyond these for another 200 m to reach a sharp right turn. Take the track, on the left, signed as part of the Wolds Way.

The ruined church, Wharram Percy

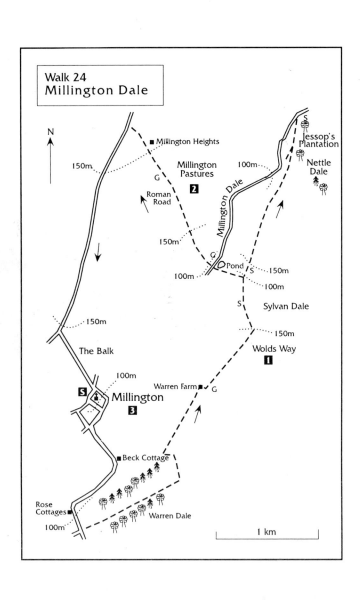

Walk 24
Millington Dale

N

150m

■ Millington Heights

Millington
Pastures
2

G

Roman
Road

150m

Millington Dale

100m

Jessop's
Plantation

Nettle
Dale

G
Pond S

150m
100m

Sylvan Dale

S

150m

Wolds Way
1

150m

The Balk

100m

Warren Farm ■ G

S Millington
3

Beck Cottage

Rose
Cottages ■

Warren Dale

100m

1 km

Follow the track, climbing steadily uphill with the woodland of Warren Dale – chiefly of ash and hawthorn – to the right. When the woodland ends, maintain direction for a short distance to where the track bears around to the left. There is a poorly positioned Wolds Way marker here. The next waymarker is much more easily seen: turn sharp left, then sharp right a little further on. The views to Millington village and Millington Bottom from here are stunning. Follow the Wolds Way to Warren Farm where it meets the North Wolds Walk and the Minster Way (see (1) Other Walks). Go to the right of the farm buildings, soon turning right and then left to follow the wold top to the edge of the aptly named Sylvan Dale. The Way bears left and descends the dale, keeping to the right of the steepest ground to reach the line of an old earthwork. The route can be shortened at this point, a footpath turning left to reach the road in Millington Dale near a delightful pond.

The best route is to continue with the Wolds Way, following the earthwork line northwards past Nettle Dale, on the right, to reach the corner of Jessop's Plantation. At the corner there is a crossroads of tracks: the Wolds Way goes right here, but we turn left, soon reaching a road.

Turn left and follow the road through Millington Dale. Despite the tarmac this is one of the finest sections of the walk. Just after passing the pond, on the left, close to the entrance to Sylvan Dale, turn right through a gate to follow a signed path that follows the course of a Roman road known locally as Thieves Sty. The path climbs steeply at first, but then more gently through Millington Pastures (see (2) Millington Pastures). Continue along the track to reach Millington Heights Farm. Follow the farm lane to reach a road and turn left. From the road there are superb views across the Vale of York and towards the Pennines. The latter are best seen in evening light when they are framed against the setting sun.

Follow the road for 2 km (1.25 miles) to reach a turning on the left for Millington. Take this, following the road (The Balk)

to the outskirts of Millington. Turn right at a crossroads to return to the church (see (3) Millington).

(1) Other Walks

So popular is Millington Dale that three long-distance footpaths traverse it. The Wolds Way is a National Trail, the other two walks being 'unofficial', though none the worse for that. The Minster Way links the minsters of York and Beverley, taking an 80 km (50 mile) route across the Wolds and the Vale of York. The North Wolds Way is a 32 km (20 mile) circular route linking Thixendale, Kirby Underdale, Bishop Wilton and Millington.

(2) Millington Pastures

Until the early 1960s the Pastures were the last section of open pasture on the Wolds. At that time the 160 hectares (over 400 acres) were unfenced and shared by walkers, picnickers and sheep. It was then decided to fence the Pastures, a move that caused a public outcry, with mass rambles in opposition to the proposal. The opposition came to nothing, the Pastures being fenced and, on the higher ground, cropped. Despite the enclosure, the Pastures are still the best link with the old agricultural methods on the Wolds.

(3) Millington

The village's Gate Inn records the old way of life on Millington Pastures. The common land was divided into 108 'gaits' or 'gates' under the care of a pasture manager. Each gate was pasturage for six sheep without lambs, or four sheep 'and their followers' (ie. their lambs), or two beasts under two years old, or one beast of two years. The 108 gates were then divided among the local farmers according to the size of their farm, among other considerations.

Millington Dale

Another link with the past is the wheel set in the pavement of the village's main street. This was used by the village blacksmith as a former for the hooping iron used on cartwheels.

The village church is unusually dedicated to St Margaret of Scotland. It was built originally in the 12th century, but has been remodelled several times in the intervening years. The south door is, perhaps, original: it is certainly late Norman, while the windows of the south and east chancel walls are believed to date from the 13th century. The church also has a leper window through which lepers could watch the service without mixing with the 'clean' congregation.

Walk 25 Flamborough Head

Flamborough Head is quite different to the coast traversed by the Cleveland Way, a jutting headland of white chalk cliffs famous for its bird life. This magnificent walk explores both the headland and historically interesting sites near by.

Walk category: Intermediate (4 hours)

Length: 15 km (9.5 miles)

Ascent: 50 m (165 ft)

Maps: Landranger Sheet 101, Pathfinder Sheet 646

Starting and finishing point: At 215694, the Danes' Dyke car-park, reached from the southern side of the B1255 Bridlington–Flamborough road.

From the car-park, head south towards the sea along a track on the eastern side of Danes' Dyke (see (1) Danes' Dyke). The route is well signed (for the beach) and the noise of the surf is usually a further guide. Close to the beach a stepped path on the left, signed as the Headland Way, leads up on to the cliff top.
   The walk from this point hardly requires much in the way of description – just follow the cliff-top path. Caution needs to be exercised however: the cliff is constantly being eroded by severe North Sea storms and sections of its edge can be precarious. After rounding Beacon Hill the walk descends steps to South Landing (see (2) South Landing), then ascends

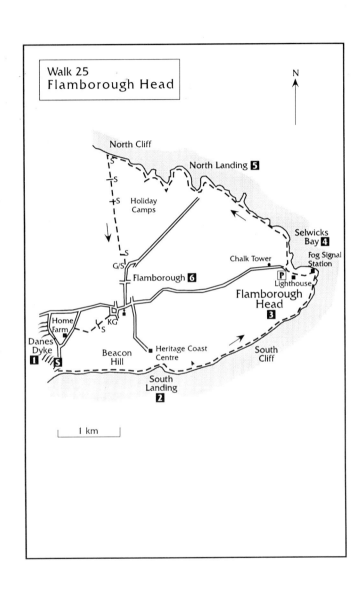

Walk 25
Flamborough Head

N

North Cliff

North Landing **5**

S
S
S
Holiday
Camps
S
G/S

Selwicks
Bay **4**

Chalk Tower

Fog Signal
Station

P Lighthouse

Flamborough **6**

Flamborough
Head
3

Home
Farm
S
KG

Danes
Dyke
1
S

Beacon
Hill

Heritage Coast
Centre

South
Cliff

South
Landing
2

1 km

to a picnic area and continues eastwards along South Cliff. The Head itself (see (3) Flamborough Head) lies close to Selwicks Bay (see (4) Selwicks Bay). Go past the fog signal station, lighthouse and coastguard station and continue between the golf course and the cliff edge.

The path cuts inland at Stottle Bank Nook, but soon regains the cliff edge. There is another coastguard station at Briel Nook before North Landing (see (5) North Landing) is reached. Here steps lead down into a gully from where a steep ascent is made to a stile over a fence. Go behind the bungalows and around another gully before resuming quiet cliff-top walking to Thornwick Bay, one of the most picturesque parts of the walk. Go past the holiday camp and continue along North Cliff, climbing steadily to reach a stile (at 224726). Cross this and turn left, inland, walking with the fence on your left. Cross two further stiles, maintaining direction and always walking close to the fence on your left, to reach a farm track. Turn left along the track for about 50 m , then go right over a stile. Now walk with the fence on your right to reach a road.

Turn right and follow the road into Flamborough (see (6) Flamborough). Go straight on at the Fishermen's Memorial, following Tower Street and then bearing right to reach the village church. Take the next turn left, then turn right into Water Lane, following it to where it turns sharply right. Here, go through the kissing gate on the left and follow a path across two fields to reach a fence. Bear right along this to reach the road from the starting car-park (the car-park has a one-way in-and-out system). Turn left to return to the start.

(1) Danes' Dyke
This dyke is a steep bank and ditch which cuts right across Flamborough Head, from coast to coast, cutting off about 13 square kilometres (5 square miles) of land. The defences are still impressive, the bank reaching a height of almost 5 m (16 ft) in places. The name refers to an ancient local legend that

it was the Danes who cut the ditch. Indeed, the area to the east of the dyke is still occasionally referred to as Little Denmark. In reality, although the Danes did settle this area (the name 'Flam' is Danish, either from the word for a headland or from the name of a chieftain), neither this earthwork nor that of Danes' Graves to the south-west of nearby Bridlington have anything to do with them. Each was constructed around the 1st century AD by Iron Age folk, although flint arrowheads found during excavations suggest that there were earlier dwellers on the headland and, perhaps, an early defensive structure, one dating from 1000 years before the now accepted date of the dyke. The fact that the ditch is merely the defence of an Iron Age fort does not, however, detract from the sheer engineering achievement of its construction. A local legend has it that the dyke is haunted by 'The White Lady', though the exact origins of the ghost are unclear.

(2) South Landing
Little now remains of the port first mentioned in 1323 when Edward II ordered its 'keepers' to deny access to a group of renegades. Above the landing, which is also home to the Flamborough lifeboat, is a Heritage Coast Centre with impressive displays on the coastal geology and natural history.

(3) Flamborough Head
The Head is chalk, a soft rock which erodes easily, forming stacks, blow-holes and sheer cliffs, all of which features are seen to perfection on this walk. The Head, together with Bempton Cliffs to the north, is one of Britain's foremost seabird nesting sites. Walkers during April, May and June will see kittiwakes, guillemots, razorbills and puffins. The Bempton Cliffs are the site of Britain's only mainland nesting colony of gannets and, as the cliffs are only a short distance north of

The chalk tower, Flamborough Head

Thornwick Bay, these birds will also be seen. The cliffs are the haunt too of corn buntings and rock pipits. During the spring and autumn the Head is a good place to watch migrating birds. The waters offshore are equally important for their wildlife, many hundreds of species inhabiting the underwater kelp forests.

(4) Selwicks Bay

The bay's name is pronounced 'silex'. It is a well-known graveyard for shipping, the fog signal station and lighthouse now warning of the dangers that doomed numerous ships in ancient times. The villagers of Flamborough helped stricken crews, but in 1779 about 1000 of them gathered for a different reason – to watch the Scottish-born American privateer John Paul Jones fight two English men-o'-war off the headland. Jones' ship was seriously damaged, so badly that one of his gunners shouted a surrender to the British. This infuriated Jones, who attempted to shoot him. When his pistol jammed Jones smashed the man over the head with it instead, killing him as he shouted 'I have not begun to fight yet.' The British were, not surprisingly, taken aback, allowing Jones to sail his ship, the *Bonhomme Richard*, close to the *Serapis* and to board and capture her. The *Bonhomme Richard* sank, but Jones escaped to Holland in the *Serapis*, taking her captain, Richard Pearson, as a prisoner.

The striking octagonal tower inland from the modern light-house is the Chalk Tower, erected in 1674 by Sir John Clayton. Although the tower is the oldest lighthouse in Britain there is dispute as to whether it ever actually served its purpose. It was intended to be lit by coal or wood, and some experts claim it operated for many years, perhaps even 100 years. Others contend that permission to erect it was only granted – by Charles II – on condition that Clayton build two more towers

Selwicks Bay

in Norfolk and Suffolk. Clayton's plan was to collect a tax from passing ships, but the other towers were not built – did Clayton run out of cash ? – and some experts contend that the Chalk Tower was, as a result, never lit.

(5) North Landing
The local lifeboat was stationed in this bay until 1993 when it was moved to its new house at South Landing. North Landing was once popular with smugglers who used caves in the cliffs for storing contraband.

(6) Flamborough
The Fishermen's Memorial passed on the walk was erected to two brothers who died in February 1909 attempting to save the crew of a ship wrecked on the treacherous local coast. The newer plaque beside the memorial commemorates the loss of ten folk when two ships floundered in May 1984.

In Tower Street, to the right, are the remains of Flamborough Castle, a 14th century pele tower. St Oswald's Church is 12th century and has an excellent 16th century rood screen and a fine, and rare, loft. There is also a monument to Sir Marmaduke Constable who died in 1520. It shows him with his heart bared, a reference to a local legend that he had swallowed a toad and died when the toad ate his heart.

The Fishermen's Memorial, Flamborough

The Vale of York

No book on Yorkshire would be complete without a walk around the city walls of York. That walk (walk 26) is included in this section. Also included is a walk around Fountains Abbey, one of the finest medieval monastic ruins in Europe (walk 27). These two walks chose themselves, as do the walks in the Dales and Moors National Parks, and on the Wolds and Pennines. But after those areas have been covered there is still a great deal of Yorkshire left. There is no good title for this area, and no easy way to choose which fine routes/places to leave out. There will be those who would have included routes near Harrogate, Northallerton, Pickering or Ripon, the battle-fields of Marston Moor or the Standard, or the geological curiosity of Spurn Head. All would be fine and worthwhile routes, but choices have to be made, and in this section on 'lowland' Yorkshire, in addition to the two routes mentioned above, we travel to Hovingham. Technically in the Vale of Pickering rather than the Vale of York, Hovingham has to live with the title 'prettiest village in Yorkshire'. That could be an embarrassment, but Hovingham carries the title well and offers a fine walk.

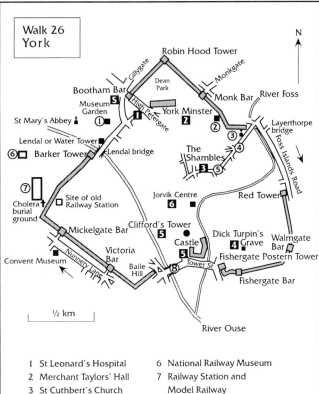

Walk 26
York

N

Robin Hood Tower

Gillygate

Monkgate

Bootham Bar

Dean
Park

Monk Bar   River Foss

Museum
Garden

High Petergate

York Minster

St Mary's Abbey

St Leonard's Hospital

York Minster

Layerthorpe
bridge

Lendal or Water Tower

Barker Tower

Lendal bridge

The
Shambles

Foss Islands Road

Cholera
burial
ground

Site of old
Railway Station

Jorvik Centre

Red Tower

Mickelgate Bar

Nunnery Lane

Victoria
Bar

Convent Museum

Clifford's Tower

Castle

Baile
Hill

Dick Turpin's
Grave

Walmgate
Bar

Tower St

Fishergate Postern Tower

Fishergate Bar

½ km

River Ouse

1 St Leonard's Hospital
2 Merchant Taylors' Hall
3 St Cuthbert's Church
4 Peasholme Green
5 The Stonebow

6 National Railway Museum
7 Railway Station and
   Model Railway
8 Skeldersgate Bridge

Walk 26 York

To do it real justice, the city of York deserves a book all to itself, history and legend oozing from virtually every stone. Here we satisfy ourselves with a walk around the city walls, from which most of the city's major sites can be glimpsed.

Walk category: Easy (1.5 hours)

Length: 4.5 kms (2.5 miles)

Ascent: 30 m (100 ft)

Maps: Town maps of York are available from the Tourist Information Centre in St Leonards Place just a few steps from the suggested start of the walk.

Starting and finishing point: Bootham Bar.

Standing outside York (as it would have been when the walls were complete) you will see steps to the right side of the gateway: climb these steps to the gate, noticing the portcullis which has now been fixed in position. Bootham Bar is the oldest of the city's existing gates, dating from the 13th century. Originally the gateway was completed by a barbican, but this was demolished in 1835. Early engravings of Bootham show the barbican to have been a superb structure, a sad loss. Bootham Bar stands above High Petergate, one of the main entrances to Roman York (see (1) York) and the first section of wall walked runs along the line of the original Roman wall. Bootham Bar is also the closest gateway to the Minster which is reached by a short walk along High Petergate (see (2) York Minster).

Walk along the old wall, with the Minster to your right. The nearer buildings are the Minster Library and Deanery, standing in Dean Park. Round the northernmost corner tower (named Robin Hood's Tower, with no justification) and head towards Monk Bar. This gateway was originally called Monkgate Bar, named for a small monastery that stood nearby. The original Roman gateway stood even closer to the monastery, the new gateway being made after repeated complaints from the monks that the road through their grounds was making their contemplative life a misery. Today Monk Bar houses a small museum dealing with Richard III. Evidence is presented to allow the visitor to choose between the conventional view of Richard (evil, crippled murderer) and one that owes less to the propaganda of his enemies. Before leaving the Bar, look out for the carved figures on the battlements of the round towers, each holding a rock in readiness to repel attackers.

Beyond Monk Bar the walk passes the 15th century Merchant Taylors Hall, to the right, and then ends close to St Cuthbert's Church – which has a magnificent 14th century timber roof. The wall originally ended at Layerthorpe Postern, but this tower was demolished in the early 19th century. Descend to Peasholme Green, from where a short detour – walk towards the city centre along Peasholme Green and The Stonebow, and then turn right – leads to The Shambles, one of York's most famous streets (see (3) The Shambles).

To continue the walk cross Layerthorpe Bridge and walk along Foss Islands Road. This is a relatively uninviting section of the walk, but the absence of wall is historically correct rather than due to demolition. In medieval times the River Foss formed a huge lake at this point, the lake providing a natural defence that was not reinforced by walling.

The wall is regained at the Red Tower, a 15th century watchtower. Its construction, in brick and tile (the brick accounting for the name) caused huge resentment among York's stonemasons and in the ensuing confrontations a tiler was killed. Red Tower is the only part of the wall not built of stone. The most interesting aspect of the tower is the lavatory that projects from its side. It takes little imagination to work out that life in medieval York was not altogether pleasant. Beyond the tower the wall reaches Walmgate Bar which retains its barbican. It is, in fact, the only surviving medieval gateway in Britain to be complete with its original barbican. The next section of wall is open as far as Fishergate Bar, one of the smaller gateways. The name derives from the fact that the outer defensive ditch on this section of the wall was once flooded and used to raise bream and pike. Fishergate Postern Tower beyond the gateway is the only one of the wall's six postern towers to survive in its original form. From it the walker must descend again, but there are several sites nearby that are worth visiting. Closest to the tower is the site of Dick Turpin's Grave (see (4) Dick Turpin), while the next part of the route goes close to York Castle (see (5) York Castle) and – just to the north – the Jorvik Viking Centre (see (6) Jorvik).

There are remnants of a section of wall close to the castle (in Tower Street), including the modified postern tower now known as Davy Tower. The next complete wall section is reached by crossing Skeldergate Bridge over the River Ouse to reach the 19th century tower at the base of Baile Hill. Baile Hill was the site of the first Norman castle at York. Go around the corner tower to reach Victoria Bar, constructed in 1837 – the year Victoria became Queen – to assist traffic flow into the city. During construction of the new gateway an old blocked gateway was discovered. On the outside of the walls here is Nunnery Lane, named for St Mary's Convent, founded in 1686 and now housing All Saints' Comprehensive School. Walkers who have completed Walk 20 might be interested in the Clitherow Museum housed in the school. Margaret Clitherow is the centre of one legend about the Lady Chapel visited on

Walk 20 (the story being that after her execution for sheltering Catholic priests her body was spirited away to the Lady Chapel for burial). A priest hole can be seen at the museum, which also has a hand of Margaret, a sacred relic.

The next gateway reached is Micklegate Bar, the name deriving from 'mickle', the old word for 'great'. It was on spikes at this gateway that the heads of traitors would be exhibited, the holes in the stonework that carried the spiked poles still being visible. The Bar houses a museum that explores the history of York and its inhabitants.

Beyond Micklegate Bar, on the inside of the walls, is the site of York's first railway station. The present station is on the outside of the walls. Here, too, is the York Model Railway, one of the best of its kind in the country, and, a little further on, the National Railway Museum. York has an enviable position in the history of railways and this is fully explored at the museum. Exhibits include the *Mallard*, the world's fastest steam engine, and Queen Victoria's royal carriage.

A less joyful example of life in old York can also be found outside the walls here. The cholera burial ground dates from 1832, a plaque marking the spot where 189 inhabitants of the city were buried after an epidemic of the disease. The final tower on this section of the wall is Barker Tower. Beyond is the River Ouse. The river was fortified by hanging a chain across it, linking Barker Tower and Lendal Tower on the far side. Lendal Tower is also known as Water Tower, the name dating from the early 17th century when an unsuccessful attempt was made to supply water to the city from the river. From Barker Tower, descend to Lendal Bridge across the Ouse, walk past Lendal Tower and bear left into Museum Gardens to follow the old line of the walls past the ruins of the medieval St Leonard's Hospital. Bear right past the Multi-angular Tower, a remnant of the Roman walls dating from about AD 300. To the left from here are the ruins of St Mary's Abbey, founded in the late 11th century for Benedictine monks and dissolved by

Henry VIII, and the Yorkshire Museum which explores the history of the county. Beyond the museum is Kings Manor, built for the abbots of St Mary's Abbey and now part of York University. The name derives from a stay by Charles I. Ahead now is Bootham Bar and the end of a fascinating walk.

(1) York

Although the site beside the Rivers Ouse and Foss was probably inhabited before the coming of the Romans, it is with Roman *Eboracum* that the city's catalogued history begins. The first Roman fort was built here in AD 71 and quickly became the centre for the pacification of the northernmost outpost of the Empire. By the 3rd century AD York had become not only the chief city of Roman Britain, but one of the most important cities of the Western Empire. In 306, during a visit to the city, the Emperor died and his son, Constantine the Great, who had accompanied his father on his visit, was proclaimed Emperor of the Western Empire.

When the Romans retreated York became the capital of the Anglian kingdom of Deira. A grammar school created during this time (the late 7th and early 8th centuries) was one of the first to have been started in Britain. When the Vikings captured York they destroyed the Anglian city, but had soon made Jorvik their own capital. The Normans built not one but two castles here and began the work of creating the walls that form the basis of this walk. Within those walls the layout and buildings of medieval York can still be found: for a real appreciation of the history of the city, the area within the walls should be explored.

(2) York Minster

In AD 627 King Edwin was baptized in a small wooden church at York, the first Christian King of Anglian Northumbria. The church was built especially for the baptism, but it is believed to have stood on the site now occupied by the Minster, giving

the site an unbroken history of over 1300 years of Christian worship. The present building dates from 1220 (though the building work lasted for 250 years) when the first Norman cathedral – built in the last years of the 11th century – was demolished. Sections of the older cathedral can still be seen in the western crypt. The completed Minster is one of the finest Gothic cathedrals in the world, a masterpiece in stone and glass. The east window is the largest surviving area of medieval glass in the world. It was created over a three-year period from 1405 by John Thornton, a glazier from Coventry, who was paid the vast sum of £58 for the work. The view along the soaring nave to the window is one of the finest in the Minster.

(3) The Shambles
The Shambles is York's oldest and most picturesque street, having been mentioned in the Domesday Book (where Robert, a half-brother of William the Conqueror, is listed as a stall-keeper). The name derives from Flesshamels, Butcher's Street, the *hamel* being the bench on which the butcher worked. Later the word shambles came to mean any scene of slaughter and was often applied to places of execution. From that usage derives the modern meaning of a mess or muddle.

(4) Dick Turpin
Turpin, born in 1706, was an Essex-based cattle rustler and deer poacher who fell into partnership with Tom King, one of the most notorious of local highwaymen. Fearing detection, in 1739 Turpin fled north under the name of John Palmer, but was arrested in York for horse-stealing. When his true identity was revealed, Turpin was condemned to death and hanged. Turpin would probably have been just another highwayman had it not been for the telling of his (exaggerated) story in the 'penny-dreadfuls' of the day. These tales romanticized his

York Minster

exploits and, specifically, his ride to York on his horse Bess, the highwayman soon becoming a popular Robin Hood-type character.

(5) York Castle

The castle complex consists of Clifford's Tower and the Castle Museum. The Tower was built in the 13th century as the keep of the Norman castle, replacing a wooden keep which had been destroyed by fire. The position is a perfect example of a Norman motte and bailey castle. The name commemorates a savage moment in the tower's history when the body of Sir Roger Clifford, a Lancastrian, was hung in chains from the walls after the battle of Boroughbridge in 1322.

The Castle Museum occupies a building that was never part of a castle but was constructed in 1701–5 as a debtors' prison using stone from St Mary's Abbey. It was in this prison that Dick Turpin was held and unmasked. Later additions to the first prison included a female prison and an assize court. Today the old prison houses a folk museum which began life in 1938 based around the collection of Dr John Kirk, a Pickering doctor. The condemned cell in which Dick Turpin reputedly spent his last days can also be seen.

(6) Jorvik

Excavations in Coppergate revealed the best-preserved domestic buildings so far found in any Viking city. These form the basis of the Jorvik Viking Centre whose innovative presentation of 10th century York has won numerous awards. Models and reconstructions allow a real appreciation of what it must have been like to live in the city at that time.

The Shambles, York

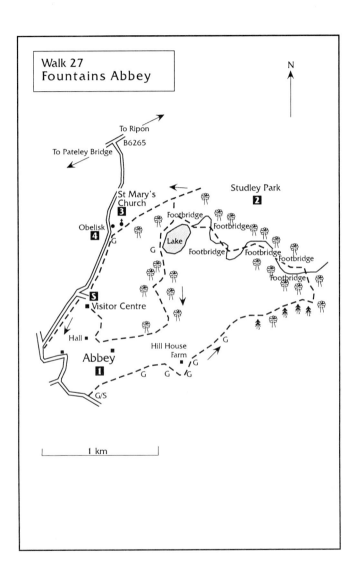

Walk 27
Fountains Abbey

N

To Ripon
B6265

To Pateley Bridge

Studley Park
2

St Mary's
Church
3

Footbridge

Footbridge

Obelisk
4

G

Lake

G

Footbridge

Footbridge

Footbridge

Footbridge

S

Visitor Centre

Hall

Hill House
Farm

G

Abbey
1

G

G

G

G/S

1 km

Walk 27 Fountains Abbey

Fountains is the most complete medieval monastic house in Britain (and one of the most complete in Europe) and is the centrepiece of the National Trust's Studley Royal Country Park. This short, easy walk explores the Park which has much of interest in addition to the abbey itself.

Walk category: Easy (1.5 hours)

Length: 7 km (4.5 miles)

Ascent: 70 m (230 ft)

Maps: Landranger Sheet 99, Pathfinder Sheet 653

Starting and finishing point: At 273685, the Visitor Centre car-park at Fountains Abbey.

From the car-park, walk back past the Visitor Centre to the roundabout and take the second exit, heading south-west along a road signed (oddly) with a triangle. Soon a signed track leaves the road on the left: take this, rejoining the road further on. Turn left and follow the road sharply left to pass other buildings of the Fountains Abbey complex, to the right. Go sharp right to cross the bridge over the River Skell and walk past the old car-park (from before the new Visitor Centre was constructed) on the right. Follow the road uphill to reach a signed stile on the left. Cross this and follow the well-way-marked path beyond, going through several gates to reach Hill House Farm. On the way to the farm there is a stunning view of the abbey (see (1) Fountains Abbey) in the valley to the left.

Keep to the right-hand side of the farm, following the waymarkers through gates and along the edge of a field. Where the hedge on your right ends, bear left, downhill, to reach a gate at the edge of woodland. Follow the woodland path beyond, with occasional views of Ripon Cathedral and the western edge of the North York Moors ahead. When the path reaches a distinct crossroads of paths, turn sharp left and descend to the River Skell. Cross the river by the ford ahead or the footbridge to the left, and turn left, following a path that enters the deer park (see (2) Studley Park) and crosses and recrosses the river several times.

Beyond the final river crossing, at the weir and lake, a distinct crossing path is reached. To return from here the walker can turn left, following the lakeside past an entrance to the abbey itself. The route continues through the beautiful parkland of Studley Royal Country Park, with its glorious array of lakes, gardens and temples, to reach a view of the abbey every bit as stunning as that on the outward leg. Follow the well-waymarked path back to the start.

An alternative route back to the start turns right along the crossing path, then left again towards the church whose spire has dominated the skyline for some distance. From the church (see (3) St Mary's Church) continue past the obelisk (see (4) Obelisk), leaving the Park through a gate in the wall and turning left along the clear track that runs parallel with the new road linking the B6265 with the Visitor Centre. When the road is reached, turn left to return to the car-park.

(1) Fountains Abbey

In 1132 a small group of monks at the Benedictine Abbey at York approached their abbot with the view that the brothers had become too lax in their observance of the rules of the founding saint: too much good food was being eaten and

The Studley Park Lake

clothes of too fine a cloth worn. In short, life had become too easy. The abbot, an old man unused to being questioned, took exception to the approach, rejecting it so forcibly that the monks went over his head to the Archbishop of York. Appalled, the abbot gathered support from other Benedictine houses – those minded, like him, to maintain the status quo – and confronted the Archbishop when he called to discuss the matter. Discussion became heated, eventually resulting in a fight in the cloister between the rival factions. The Archbishop had little choice but to seek sanctuary in the church together with the group of disillusioned monks. Convinced of the merits of their case by the fracas, the Archbishop then took the dissenters to a wild, never cultivated stretch of land beside the River Skell and invited them to found a house of their own. The site was uninviting, but did have a nearby supply of good water from springs on the hillside. These springs, or fountains, gave the new abbey its name.

For several years the Fountains monks – who had chosen the Cistercian order – hovered on the verge of starvation, but, eventually, they received several endowments from rich land-owners, who were seeking to ease their own paths to heaven, and building work began. By the mid-13th century Fountains was one of the richest Cistercian houses in Britain with vast holdings of land, the produce from which created wealth which was supplemented by the sale of wool from the thousands of sheep the monks bred on the neighbouring hills. It is thought that there were as many as 600 lay-brethren (non-monks who did the manual labour for the house) working on Fountains' properties. Some of these may have been the menfolk from hamlets the Fountains monks evicted to increase the abbey's income, a curiously unchristian approach to tenants that made Fountains unpopular, but increased its wealth still further. Bad management reduced the abbey's prosperity, but by the time of the Dissolution Fountains had regained its position of power and wealth. In 1536 Thomas Cromwell replaced Abbot William Thirsk, Cromwell considering him to be unsympathetic towards Henry VIII's position over his marriage to Catherine of Aragon. Cromwell was correct, Thirsk's support for the Pilgrimage of Grace (from his 'retirement' at Jervaulx Abbey) leading to his execution in 1537. But Cromwell's appointed successor at Fountains, Abbot Marmaduke Bradley, was no more pliable. Bradley escaped execution and, indeed, was retired on a handsome pension, but was forced to surrender Fountains on 26 November 1539. It was the richest Cistercian house in Britain at the time, with an income of over £1000 annually and silverware of staggering value.

It was normal practice for dissolved abbeys to be used as a quarry by the locals, but at Fountains the remoteness of the site means that the buildings are surprisingly intact. The roofs and windows have gone, and time has taken its toll on the structure, but enough survives to give a real insight into the nature of medieval monasticism. The church, with its huge east window, is magnificent. The tower, over 50 m (165 ft) high, stands, unusually, above the north transept. It was added in the late 15th/early 16th century by Abbot Huby – one of Fountains' most successful abbots – who chose that position after the disastrous attempts to increase the heights of central towers at Shap and Furness.

The remaining buildings are too extensive to attempt a detailed description, but visitors should find time to admire the vaulting in the cellarium, and the marvellous sweep of the monks' day stairs.

(2) Studley Park
After the Dissolution, there was a plan to convert Fountains
into a cathedral, but nothing came of this and in 1540 the site
was sold to Sir Richard Gresham. Gresham's descendants sold
it to Stephen Proctor whose father had made a fortune in iron.
Proctor used stone from the abbey to build Fountains Hall and
improved the deer park that the Greshams had created. Ultimately the site passed to John Aislabie who was Chancellor of
the Exchequer at the time of the South Sea Bubble scandal of
1720. Aislabie was implicated and imprisoned, and, on his
release, returned to Fountains where he devoted his energies
to improving the Deer Park, with its gardens, lakes and
temples, and the state of the abbey buildings. Thankfully, some
of Aislabie's 'picturesque additions' to the abbey ruins were
demolished in later centuries. Those walkers who use the
lakeside return route to the start are treated to a marvellous
view of the abbey, Aislabie having laid out his gardens for just
that reason. Those on the alternative return view Aislabie's
entrance drive from Studley Roger. The drive was laid out to
align exactly with the towers of Ripon Cathedral.

(3) St Mary's Church
The church was built in 1870 by William Burges for the Marquis
of Ripon who owned the Park after the Aislabies, and it is now
recognized as Burges' masterpiece. Its position was chosen so
that visitors on the entrance drive would have views of Ripon
Cathedral at one end and the distinctive church spire at the
other.

(4) Obelisk
The original construction here was a wooden funerary pyramid
erected by William Aislabie in 1742 as a memorial to his father.
The present obelisk, which has no inscription, dates from 1805.

Walk 28 Hovingham

There is strong competition for the title 'prettiest village in Yorkshire', but Hovingham features towards the head of most lists. This walk explores the village and the delightful country to the south, using a section of the Ebor Way to return.

Walk category: Easy/Intermediate (2 hours)

Length: 7.5 kms (4.75 miles)

Ascent: 70 m (230 ft)

Maps: Landranger Sheet 100, Pathfinder Sheet 643

Starting and finishing point: Parking is possible, but limited, in Hovingham (try close to the Green, on its church side). It is easier to use the verge beside the road at 656753.

From the verge parking at 656753, go along the signed path that leaves the road on its southern side (not the wider track that leaves the road a little closer to Hovingham), walking though fine woodland with a stream murmuring to your left. Follow the stream out of the wood and continue beside it, crossing fields linked by a gate.

The stream is followed to the approach road to Hovingham Lodge. Turn left along the road, turning sharp right, and then going around a sharp left-hand bend to pass the Lodge (on your left). Follow the access road downhill (passing a house on the right patrolled by a frantic but, apparently, harmless dog) and then uphill to reach a sharp right-hand turning. There, go

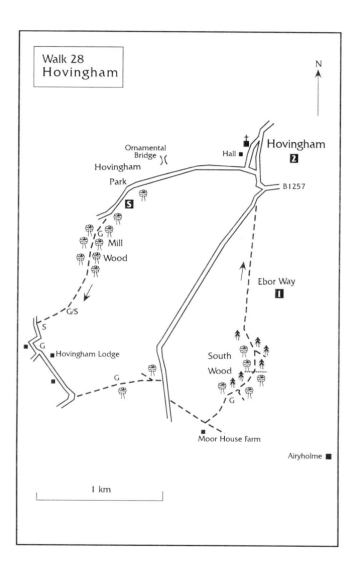

Walk 28
Hovingham

N

Ornamental
Bridge)(
Hovingham
Park

S

Mill
Wood

G/S

S
G
■ Hovingham Lodge

G

G

■

Hovingham

Hall ■

2

B1257

Ebor Way

1

South
Wood

G

■ Moor House Farm

Airyholme ■

1 km

left to follow a track downhill. Go through a gate at the valley bottom and follow a path overgrown with bracken to reach a road. Turn right along the road for 200 m, then turn left along the track signed for Airyholme.

Follow the track to Moor House Farm where an unsigned, but obvious, track goes sharp left (at the name sign for the farm) downhill towards South Wood. Go through a gate into the wood and follow the path beyond uphill. The path joins a broad 'ride' coming in from the right: continue along the ride. When a crossing ride is reached, continue ahead, bearing left when another track joins from the right to walk past a pond and exit the wood. The section of the walk through the wood and into Hovingham is part of the Ebor Way (see (1) Ebor Way), though the Way is poorly signed. Follow a track across fine country, going over a shallow ridge to reveal Hovingham below. Descend towards the village to reach a road. Turn right and follow the road towards its junction with the B1257, but cross and take a paved path that cuts off the corner.

Turn second left along Park Street, with the green on your right, and then first right to visit the church, passing Hovingham Hall (see (2) Hovingham). From the church walk back to Park Street and turn right, soon going between pillars that mark the boundary of the village. In ancient times there was a gate between the pillars, the village children charging travellers for opening it. Follow the road through a one-sided avenue (trees on your left), chiefly of oak at first and then of horse chestnut and past an elegant bridge in the middle of the field on the right. The bridge, called Pickering Bridge, once stood at the head of an ornamental lake in the Hall's park and presumably then looked much less out of place. Continue along the road to regain the start.

(1) Ebor Way
This 112 km (70 mile) waymarked trail takes its name from Roman York – Eboracum. As might be expected, the city is traversed by the route on its way from Ilkley to Helmsley.

(2) Hovingham
With its Hall, church, cluster of stone houses, tree-framed green and stream Hovingham is both picturesque and the epitome of Englishness. It is no surprise that the grounds of the Hall include an excellent cricket pitch or that a former owner, Sir William Worsley – father of the Duchess of Kent – captained Yorkshire. The Hall was built in 1760 by Sir Thomas Worsley, Surveyor-General to George III, though the land had been in the Worsley family for at least two centuries. The Hall is in Palladian style and was built in the local yellow sandstone. During the landscaping of the Hall's grounds the remains of a Roman villa were uncovered, coins dating its occupancy from about AD 90 to AD 300. It is likely that the Romans were attracted by the thermal springs to the west of the village. In Victorian times an attempt was made to create a spa to rival Harrogate (the Worsley Hall Hotel having been built to accommodate spa visitors) but the venture failed. The Ebor Way passes the remaining spa buildings on its way to Cawton.

The village's beautiful school was built in 1864, the equally delightful School House beside it having been built for the first teacher.

The west tower of Hovingham's All Saints' Church is late Saxon, one of very few in Yorkshire. The west doorway is also Saxon and has an Anglian cross carved above it. The remainder of the church dates from a substantial rebuilding in 1860. Inside there is a carved Saxon stone, possibly a lintel or altar from the original Saxon church, the carvings representing figures from Christ's life, and a 10th century carved cross.

The village green, Hovingham

The Pennines

The invading Romans, noting the similarity between the central upland backbone of England and their own Apennines, gave the uplands the same name. That, at least, is the story. In reality the name was given to the hills as recently as 1747 when Charles Bertram, the young Professor of English at the University of Copenhagen, claimed to have discovered an ancient manuscript. This manuscript, *De Statu Britanniae*, was, Bertram said, written by a 14th century monk and stated that *Alpes Penina* was the name used by the Romans to describe England's upland backbone. In practice there was no such manuscript and Bertram's claim, as with many of his other Roman names, was fraudulent. The only early reference to the name is in the work of Camden, published in 1586, which notes that the uplands 'like the Apennine in Italy, ran through the middle of England in one continued ridge'.

Notwithstanding the fact that the story was invented, the name stuck. In 1822 the geologists Conybeare and Phillips turned the name around, writing Penine Alps. The Alps was soon dropped and, taking their cue from the Italian range, Penine soon became Pennine.

England's Pennines are a long, narrow upland mass, stretching for some 240 km (about 150 miles) from Stoke/Derby to the Tyne Valley. The upland mass is never more than 60 km (about 40 miles) wide, and frequently only 30 km (about 20 miles) wide. At its southern end the chain is encompassed by the Peak National Park. In Yorkshire the Pennines are encompassed by the Yorkshire Dales National Park. Between these two parks the hills are squeezed between the industrial heartlands of Lancashire and Yorkshire. Here, too, they are at their lowest, despite being composed of a slab of tough Millstone Grit.

The two routes described here visit this less well-known area of the Pennines, and illustrate that despite the closeness of urban sprawl and the lack of height the area has much to offer.

Walk 29 Haworth

No book on Yorkshire walks would be complete without a route on the southern Pennines, and no collection of walks in that area could ignore the Brontës. This walk starts at Haworth, the family home, and reaches Top Withins, long held to be the model for Wuthering Heights. The walk is well signed as far as Top Withins: indeed, it must be the only route in Yorkshire whose signs are in Japanese as well as English, so popular is the literary pilgrimage to the ruined farm.

Walk category: Intermediate (4 hours)

Length: 14 km (8.5 miles)

Ascent: 275 m (900 ft)

Maps: Landranger Sheets 103 and 104, Outdoor Leisure Sheet 21

Starting and finishing point: At 030372, the Brontë Parsonage Museum in Haworth. There are several car-parks in Haworth, any of which can be used. There are also several other car-parks in the Country Park on Penistone Hill to the west of the town. These offer alternative starts or the option of shortening the walk.

From the museum (see (1) Brontë Parsonage Museum), take the path that runs between it and the church. Continue along the paved track, then turn first right along a lane past Balcony Farm to reach a road. Go straight across to reach a path fork.

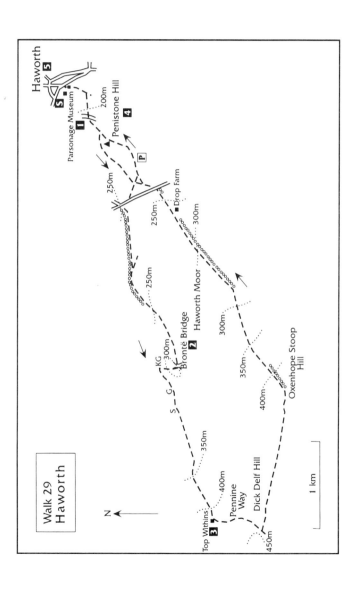

Walk 29
Haworth

N

Haworth

5

5

Parsonage Museum

1

200m

Penistone Hill

4

P

250m

Drop Farm

250m

300m

250m

Haworth Moor

Bronté Bridge

2

300m

KG

300m

G

S

250m

350m

300m

350m

400m

Oxenhope Stoop
Hill

Top Withins

3

400m

Pennine Way

Dick Delf Hill

450m

1 km

Take the left-hand branch (the Brontë Way), climbing to reach another fork. Here, take the right-hand branch, contouring below the summit of Penistone Hill – the top is visited on the return route – and passing a car-park to reach a path junction. Turn right, as signed for the Brontë Way, and follow the path to a road.

Turn right, but soon, where another road goes off right, turn left along a moorland track. The track, another section of the Brontë Way, follows the wall on the right until it turns away, then descends to Brontë Bridge (see (2) Brontë Bridge). Cross and ascend to a kissing gate. Go through and turn left. The path now follows the broken wall on the left, passing through other broken walls, to reach the elbow of an intact wall on the right. Follow this wall to a squeeze gate. Cross and maintain direction to reach a stile in the wall ahead. Cross and follow the clear path beyond. The path runs parallel to South Dean Brook, to your left, going through an old wall and then crossing an infeed stream using long striding stepping stones. Beyond there is a short, steep – but part-paved – climb to reach the Pennine Way and Top Withins (see (3) Top Withins).

From Top Withins the Pennine Way is now followed southwards, the Way part-paved as it climbs to the watershed ridge between the shallow rises of Round Hill to the right, and Dick Delf Hill, to the left. The latter is the next objective: when the ridge top is reached, keep ahead, then at its far side, turn left to follow an indistinct path beside a drain. Follow the path over the top of Dick Delf Hill and along the broad ridge towards Oxenhope Stoop Hill. The path goes to the right of the actual summit (though the difference is hardly noticeable) to reach the corner of a broken wall with a view of modern windmills to the right ahead. Bear left to walk with the wall on your right. Maintain direction when a small beck runs beside the wall, ignoring paths to both the left and the right.

The wall on the right is more complete now: follow the path as it moves towards it, then bear left, away from the wall, to

cross a beck. The path is boggy in places and occasionally runs through tall bracken, but is always obvious. Continue along it to reach Drop Farm, on the right, where at the right time of day (afternoon) refreshments are available. There is also a car-park here which can be used as an alternative start to the walk. Continue along the farm track to reach a road. Turn left along the road, but soon go right along a track towards Penistone Hill. Take the right-hand branch at a path fork, following the path as it passes yet another car-park and swings left to reach the top of the hill (see (4) Penistone Hill). Continue along the path, which descends from the summit to reach a path fork passed earlier on the route. From here, reverse the outward route back to Haworth (see (5) Haworth).

(1) Brontë Parsonage Museum

In 1820 an Irish clergyman became the parson of Haworth, taking up residence in the parsonage. He had been born Patrick Brunty, though his ancestors had probably been called O'Prunty, but had taken the name Brontë in 1799 when Lord Nelson, a great hero of the parson, had been made Duke of Brontë. Patrick had married a Cornish Methodist, Maria Branwell, late in life and they had six children in quick succession, all of them born before the family arrived in Haworth. In 1821 Maria died, probably of cancer, leaving the infant family to be brought up by her sister, Elizabeth Branwell, who travelled up from Penzance to act as a surrogate mother.

Of the children, the two eldest died in early childhood, leaving three daughters – Charlotte, Emily and Anne, the youngest child, and a son, Patrick Branwell, the fourth child. The children attended a boarding school at Cowan Bridge, a school which added to the distress they must have felt at the loss of their mother. Discipline was harsh, as were the general conditions, and it is likely that the two eldest girls died as a

Brontë Bridge

result of illnesses contracted at the school or exacerbated by conditions there. The remaining children returned home, but even there conditions were not ideal. Neither Patrick Brontë nor Aunt Branwell seems to have been affectionate and Patrick was most definitely not a social man. As a result, the three girls and Branwell were left on their own for much of the time. They spent this time roaming the moors – Emily, in particular, became passionately fond of Haworth Moor – alone with their collective imaginations.

The children invented fantasy worlds, Angria and Gondal, peopling them with characters for whom they created adventure. To such an extent was this fantasy world a part of their lives that references to it, and the development of story lines, are interspersed with the mundane happenings of everyday life in their diaries and early writings. The creation of new characters and stories continued throughout their adult lives, the vividness of the stories and the imaginative sweeps they required ultimately being translated into their serious writings.

Those writings are surprisingly few in number. Charlotte published *Jane Eyre* in October 1847. It was well received and she achieved status as a writer in her own lifetime. She published two further works, *Shirley* and *Villette* (a fourth, *The Professor*, her first novel, was published after her death: a fifth, *Miss Miles* or *Sarah Miles*, will be added to the list if the novel, published in 1890 under the name of novelist Mary Taylor, is finally acknowledged as a Charlotte Brontë work. At present experts are divided over its authenticity.). Charlotte was the only one of the children to marry, marrying her father's curate, the Rev. Nicholls, in 1854. The marriage was happy, but short, Charlotte dying in 1855 after catching a chill while walking on Haworth Moor. Charlotte had outlived all the other children. Branwell had died in September 1848, a sad young man whose final years saw him overcome by illness brought on by alcohol-

Top Withins

ism and drug abuse. He died unfulfilled, his literary and artistic abilities (he was a good portrait painter) having failed to create anything of note. In his last years he was a railway clerk. Anne died of tuberculosis in early 1849 at the age of twenty-nine. She had published *Agnes Gray* in 1847, a book that had also been well received, and *The Tenant of Wildfell Hall* in the spring of 1849 just before she died. She died in Scarborough having gone there for a sea-air cure for her illness. She is the only Brontë not buried in Haworth churchyard. Emily also died of tuberculosis, in December 1848. Patrick Brontë survived all of his children, living to be eighty-four years old.

(2) Brontë Bridge

This delightful little clapper-bridge just about deserves its name as the Brontë children almost certainly crossed it and such bridges do occur in their writings. The bridge was replaced in 1990 after a flash flood destroyed the original. The Brontë Waterfall to the south of the bridge is said to have been the target of Charlotte Brontë's last walk on the moors. As Charlotte was the last of the Brontë children it must have been a poignant trip.

(3) Top Withins

Emily Brontë wrote just one book, *Wuthering Heights*, published two months after Charlotte's *Jane Eyre* and a year before her death from tuberculosis at the age of thirty. The book was not well received at the time, taking many years to be seen as the work of genius that literary circles now consider it. Its central element is the house of the same name. As Emily herself notes in the book, 'wuthering' is 'a significant provincial adjective, descriptive of the atmospheric tumult to which its station is exposed in stormy weather'. The ruined farm – now more generally referred to as Withins as the farms of Withins and Lower Withins are no more than piles of stones – is in exactly the right spot for such a name, though in every other respect it bears no resemblance to the house in the book. The plaque on the ruin (note the odd spelling of Withins as Withens) makes this point, though its grudging acceptance of the fact that the farm might have been the model for Wuthering Heights does not fit with the feel of the place. Given the novel's dark story and sinister overtones, Withins – especially on a stormy day with the wind ripping across the moor – feels absolutely correct. In the same way, Ponden Hall, which also sits beside the Pennine Way in the valley to the north, seems to fit Thrushcross Grange. In the book, the Earnshaws lived at Wuthering Heights, and the Lintons at Thrushcross Grange, the story revolving around the passionate, obsessive relationship between Catherine Earnshaw and Heathcliff, her adopted brother.

(4) Penistone Hill
The old quarries that ate away at the slopes of the hill are now car-parks for the Country Park centred on the summit. The views from the hill are marvellous, especially those to Haworth and Haworth Moor.

(5) Haworth
Haworth would be a pleasant village even if it weren't for the Brontës, but seems overwhelmed by the family. The Black Bell is where Branwell drank himself to oblivion, the Old Apothecary is where he bought his opium and there is a stained glass window to Charlotte in the church. Only the west tower of the church would now be recognized by the family, though, the remainder having been rebuilt in 1880.

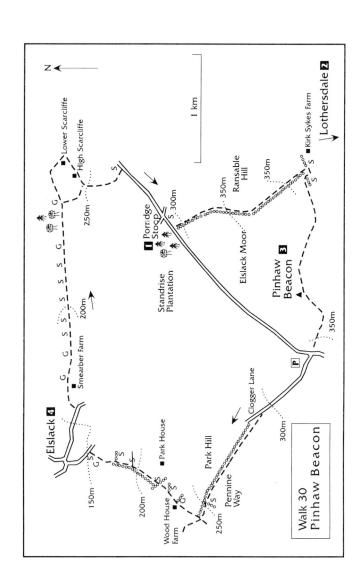

N ←

1 km

Lower Scarcliffe
■ High Scarcliffe

250m

S

← Porridge Stoop 1

S 300m

Standrise Plantation

Elslack Moor

350m

Ransable Hill

350m

■ Kirk Sykes Farm

Lothersdale 2

→

Pinhaw Beacon 3
▲

350m

Smearber Farm ■

200m

Elslack 4

150m

Park House ■

200m

Wood House Farm ■

Park Hill

Pennine Way

250m

Clogger Lane

P

300m

Walk 30
Pinhaw Beacon

Walk 30 Pinhaw Beacon

Our second route on the south Pennines visits a modest summit which, because of its position, offers panoramic views.

Walk category: Intermediate (3.5 hours)

Length: 11 km (7 miles)

Ascent: 330 m (1100 ft)

Maps: Landranger Sheet 103, Outdoor Leisure Sheet 21

Starting and finishing point: At 930493, at the centre of the hamlet of Elslack. There is also a car-park at 939472 beside the moorland road that crosses Elslack Moor. There is limited verge parking in Elslack: please park carefully and with consideration.

Leave the village along Moor Lane, the minor road to Lothersdale. After about 600 m, take the track on the left to Smearber Farm. Cross the farmyard and go through a gate. Follow the wall on the right, but where this bears away to the right, maintain direction to reach a gate in the wall ahead. The route now maintains direction across a series of moorland fields linked by stiles, following a fence, and then a wall on the left at first, then crossing a field and following a wall on the right across three more fields. At the end of the last of these, turn right through a gate and immediately left along the wall. Eventually a gate is reached in the wall (i.e. on your left). Custom and practice ignore this gate, continuing with the wall

on the left to reach the ruin of High Scarcliff. This is not, however, a right of way. That goes through the gate and turns right along the wall to reach a farm track at a cattle grid. Turn right and follow the track over two further cattle grids, passing Lower Scarcliff on the right. Just beyond the third cattle grid, turn right along a wall to reach High Scarcliff.

From the ruin head south to reach a wall and bear left along it to reach a stile on to a road. Turn right and follow the road to a crossroads (see (1) Porridge Stoop). Go straight over at the crossroads but, after a further 120 m, turn left over a stile and follow the wall on the right uphill on to Elslack Moor. The wall dog-legs twice: stay with it, crossing Ransable Hill and then descending off the moor towards Lothersdale (see (2) Lothersdale). On the other side of the wall there are a large number of grouse shooting butts.

When the wall meets another close to Kirk Sykes Farm, go over a stile and turn right to reach, very soon, another stile on the right. You have now joined the Pennine Way. Cross the stile and follow the wall on the left. Soon the Way breaks away from the wall heading up across the moor to the summit beacon of Pinhaw (see (3) Pinhaw Beacon). Follow the clear path south-westwards from the beacon bearing right to reach a road at a T-junction. The alternative starting point for the walk is to the right.

Go straight across at the junction, following the minor road downhill for about 600 m to reach a track on the left. Follow the Pennine Way down this track, walking with a wall on your right to reach a stile in the wall ahead. Cross and continue, to descend, still with a wall on your right. Go over a stile in another facing wall. Continue with the wall on your right until a footbridge which crosses both it and a beck is reached. Turn right here, across the bridge, leaving the Pennine Way which continues to descend north-westwards to Thornton-in-Craven.

Porridge Stoop

After crossing the bridge, go straight across the field ahead to reach a gate in a wall close to Wood House Farm (to your left). Go through and turn half-right along a wall (with it on your left) to reach a stile over the wall. Cross this and the field beyond to reach another stile. Go over and follow the wall on the left, crossing two further stiles. Just beyond the second of these, turn right, away from the wall, and cross to a gate and, beyond, a stile on to a road. Turn left and follow the road back to Elslack (see (4) Elslack).

(1) Porridge Stoop
This old signpost is dated 1730 and marked the junction of two important roads across the moors south-west of Skipton. It is inscribed with distances and a friendly guiding hand on all four sides.

(2) Lothersdale
It would be interesting to know how many inhabitants of this delightful little dale know that the name derives from the old English *loddere* meaning a vagabond.

(3) Pinhaw Beacon
Although reaching only 388 m (1,273 ft) Pinhaw is the highest peak for many miles north and south and offers extensive views. To the south-west are Pendle Hill in Lancashire, the Ribble Valley and the Bowland Fells. North-west are Ingleborough and Pen-y-ghent, north is Fountains Fell and north-east are Malham, Buckden Pike, Great Whernside, Earl's Scout and Simon Seat. Closer is the Aire Valley, the next objective for walkers on the Pennine Way. The Way can also be traced southwards towards Earl Crag and Ickornshaw Moor.

The grouse shooting butts beside the walk and the frequent 'private' notices of the Elslack Estate Co. indicate a usage for the moors entirely different from that of walkers, and one which created confusion and upset even after the Pennine Way had been officially designated. Walkers complained that the owners were querying the existence of a right of way and objecting to them crossing the moor. Notices were erected supporting the objections and both the County Council and the Countryside Commission became involved before the dispute was settled.

(4) Elslack

Despite its size and its somewhat straggling form, Elslack is the typical English village, a small group of picturesque houses surrounding a green. Now lost in a fold of the hills, this spot was once important, the Romans building a fort here beside their road from Ribchester to Ilkley.

Appendix 1 Other Walks in Yorkshire

Pennine Way

The Pennine Way traverses the Pennine uplands and the Yorkshire Dales National Park on its 400 km (250 mile) route from Edale to Kirk Yetholm, a village just inside Scotland, on the northern flank of the Cheviot. The route was opened in 1965, Britain's first National Trail, its creation marking the end of a long period of dispute over access to grouse moors and other unfenced upland. It is, therefore, not only the grandfather of all Trails, but a symbol of the walker's right to explore Britain's high ground. Many of the walks described in this book touch or include sections of the Way, a tribute to the excellence of its routing. Unfortunately the passage of admiring walkers has led to serious erosion on parts of the Way, the efforts to control this leading, in turn, to grumbles about overuse, the need for rationing and the merits of artificial paths. There has even been a drift away from the perceived artificiality of such Trails. Those are issues for other places and times. Suffice to say that the Pennine Way is a magnificent route through memorable scenery.

See *A Guide to the Pennine Way*, Christopher John Wright, Constable Guide.

Cleveland Way

The Cleveland Way lies wholly within Yorkshire, following the edge of the North York Moors from Helmsley to the coast near Saltburn and then following the coast southwards to Filey, a journey of about 160 km (100 miles). Although it follows the moorland edge, this fine route – another National Trail – explores many of the Moors' most interesting spots – Rievaulx

Abbey, Osmotherley and Roseberry Topping. The section of coast it then follows is arguably the finest on England's eastern coastline. Several of the walks described here touch or follow sections of the Way.

To turn the route into a full circle, the Tabular Hills Link has been waymarked from Scarborough to Helmsley. This link omits the last section of coast walking to Filey, but has the advantage of exploring the Moors' most southerly upland block.

See *A Guide to the Cleveland Way*, Richard Sale, Constable.

Wolds Way

This third National Trail also lies wholly within Yorkshire (now that Humberside north of the Humber has been returned to its rightful owner). The 130 km (80 mile) route starts near the Humber Bridge, where it links with the Viking Way, and finishes at Filey, where it links with the Cleveland Way. The route follows the Wolds' highest ridge, which runs along the area's western edge.

After the rugged delights of the Pennine Way and the Cleveland Way, the Wolds Way offers a quieter, more pastoral route. Its highlights include the scenically superb Millington Dale and the historically fascinating Wharram Percy, a deserted medieval village, both of which are visited by the walks described here.

Other Walks

Yorkshire has a great number of fine unofficial long-distance walks, some of which are mentioned in the main text when the described walks touch or follow them. The best of these are:

The *Brontë Way*, a short (40 km – 25 mile) route around Haworth Moor named for the Brontë sisters whose writings were, in part, inspired by the local scenery.

The *Coast-to-Coast Walk*, linking the west coast to Robin Hood's Bay by way of the Lakes, Yorkshire Dales and North York Moors National Parks. Because it was devised by Wainwright the route has acquired an almost mystical reputation, but there have been problems because of his decision to deviate from official rights of way.

The *Dales Way*, a 130 km (80 mile) route linking the dales of western Yorkshire, the Howgill Fells and the south-eastern Lake District.

The *Derwent Way*, which follows the River Derwent from its source on the North York Moors to its confluence with the River Ouse. This excellent 145 km (90 mile) route crosses the Vales of York and Pickering and passes Stamford Bridge and the Howardian Hills – something for everybody.

The *Ebor Way*, taking its name from Roman York (Eboracum) and passing through the city on its 110 km (70 mile) way from Helmsley, at the edge of the North York Moors, to Ilkley.

The *Eskdale Way*, a 130 km (80 mile) route that follows the river from the North York Moors to Whitby but with occasional wide arcs to savour the delights of such places as Goathland. A fine walk through varied scenery.

The *Minster Way*, linking the Minsters of York and Beverley. The 80 km (50 mile) route has scenery ranging from pastoral to high moorland and passes several places of historical interest.

The *Ribble Way*, which follows the river from its source to the sea. The 100 km (70 mile) route starts in limestone country, then descends into the fertile coastal plain and finishes by crossing tidal marshes, an excellent variety of scenery.

The *Yoredale Way*, taking its title from the old name for the River Ure, which it follows from its source to the Ouse at York. The 160 km (100 mile) route goes through the northern Yorkshire Dales before crossing the Vale of York.

In addition to the above long-distance (apart from the Brontë Way) routes, Yorkshire also has two challenge walks, that is, routes which traditionally must be completed in a defined time:

The *Lyke Wake Walk* crosses the North York Moors from west to east, starting near Scarth Nick and finishing at the sea near Ravenscar, a distance of 65 km (40 miles). The challenge is to complete the route within 24 hours.

By tradition, the *Three Peaks Walk* starts and ends at the Pen-y-ghent Café in Horton-in-Ribblesdale, reaching the summits of Pen-y-ghent, Whernside and Ingleborough in a 40 km (25 mile) circuit that must be completed within 12 hours.

For each of the walks there are badges etc. for those who complete in the allotted time. Each of these walks is superb, but the very fact of the challenge has led to huge numbers of walkers with consequent erosion problems on the paths. There have been attempts to dissuade walkers from completing the routes, and alternative paths have been opened to relieve pressure on the most eroded sections. It is not easy to identify a long-term solution: each of the walks is excellent, and it would be sad if they were 'closed', but as the scarring destroys the beauty the walkers are seeking something may have to be done.

Walks for the Disabled

Of the walks in this book, only Aysgarth Falls (as far as the falls themselves, but not the return route) and the sections of the Malham walk as far as the Cove and from the road into Gordale Scar can comfortably be followed in wheelchairs. The Bride Stones walk could be followed, but does involve steep climbs and a return across grass. However, both the Dales and the Moors National Park authorities are constantly looking to expand facilities for disabled visitors and walks are increasing in number. Please ask at the Park offices for details of recent additions to the list.

Appendix 2 Transport and Weather

Over such a large area it is not possible to be definitive about transport that is or will be available. The local information centres will have such information.

A weather report for the Yorkshire area can be obtained by dialling 0891 500418. For specific reports for the Dales and Moors it is best to ring the tourist information centres, though walkers on the Dales often find it more useful to hear the Lake District weather report on 017687 75757.

Appendix 3 Useful Addresses

Yorkshire Dales National Park
National Park Office
Colvend
Hebden Road
Grassington
BD23 5LB
Tel: 01756 752748

INFORMATION CENTRES

Aysgarth Falls
Aysgarth
Tel: 01969 663424

Clapham
Tel: 015242 51419

Hebden Road
Grassington
Tel: 01756 752774

Dales Countryside Museum
Station Road
Hawes
Tel: 01969 667450

Malham
Tel: 01729 830363

Main Street
Sedbergh
Tel: 01539 620125

North York Moors National Park
National Park Office
The Old Vicarage
Bondgate
Helmsley
Y06 5BP
Tel: 01439 70657

INFORMATION CENTRES

Danby Lodge
Danby
Tel: 01287 660540

Sutton Bank
Nr Thirsk
Tel: 01845 597426

Yorkshire Tourist Board
312 Tadcaster Road
York
YO2 2HF
Tel: 01904 707961

York City Tourist Office
6 Rougier Street
York
YO2 1JA
Tel: 01904 620557

There is also an information office in St Leonards Place near
Bootham Bar.

Council for National Parks
45 Shelton Road
London WC2H 9HJ
Tel: 0171 240 3603

Countryside Commission
John Dower House
Crescent Place
Cheltenham
GL30 3RA
Tel: 01242 521381

English Heritage
Northern Office
Bessie Surtees House
41–44 Sandhill
Newcastle-upon-Tyne
NE1 3JF
Tel: 0191 261 1585

National Trust
Yorkshire Regional Office
Goddards
27 Tadcaster Road
Dringhouses
York YO2 2QG
Tel: 01904 702021

Yorkshire Wildlife Trust
10 Toft Green
York
Tel: 01904 659570

Ramblers' Association
1/5 Wandsworth Road
London SW8 2XX
Tel: 0171 582 6878

Youth Hostels Association
Trevelyan House
St Albans
Hertfordshire
AL1 2DY
Tel: 01727 55215

Index

Aire, River, 91, 99
Aire Valley, 284
Airehead, 99
Angram Reservoir, 127
Ann's Cross on Tumulus, 204, 207
Arkengarthdale, 135
Arncliffe, 98, 103, 104, 107
Ashberry Hill, 143
Aysgarth, 49, 51, 55 see also Aysgarth
    Falls
Aysgarth Falls
    walk, 20, 48–55, 291; 52
    waterfalls, 49–50, 51, 53; 52

Barden Bridge, 116–7
Barden Tower, 117, 120–1
Batty Green, 87
Baugh Fell, 39
Bay Town , 209, 217, 219 see also Robin
    Hood's Bay
Baysdale Abbey, 189
Beck Head, 82
Beck Hole, 180
Beezley Falls, 58, 62
Beldi Hill lead mines, 135
Bempton Cliffs, 237
Beverley Minster, 231, 289
Bilsdale East Moor, 149
Bishop Wilton, 231
Black Moor, 131
Blakey Howe, 185
Blakey Topping, 179
Blea Moor Tunnel, 87, 89
Boggle Hole, 211, 219
Bolton Abbey
    Bolton Abbey and the Strid walk,
        21, 114–21; 118
    village, 115, 119; see also Bolton
        Priory

Bolton Castle, 50, 53–4
Bolton Priory, 105, 115, 117, 119, 120
Borrowby Dale, 162
Boroughbridge, 24
Bosworth Field, 28
Boulby, 162
Bow Bridge, 141
Bowland Fells, 284
Bowness-on-Windermere, 120
Brackenbottom, 71
Brants Gill Head, 75
Bride Stones walk, 19, 147–51, 291;
    150
Bridestones Griff, 149
Bridestones Nature Reserve, 149, 151
Bridge End, 107
Bridlington, 237
Brigflatts, 39
Brontë Bridge, 273, 278; 274
Brontë Parsonage Museum, 271,
    275–8
Brontë Waterfall, 278
Brontë Way, 273, 288, 290
Buckden Pike, 75, 284
Burton Howe, 23
Byland Abbey, 127, 173

Caperby, 49, 53
Captain Cook's Monument, 153, 155,
    157; 156
Carlisle see Settle to Carlisle Railway
Carlton-in-Cleveland, 151
Carlton Moor, 23
Castle Bolton see Bolton Castle
Cautley Holme Beck, 37
Cautley Spout, 19, 36–40; 38
Cavendish Memorial, 117, 121
Cawthorn, 26, 179
Cawton, 267

Chalk Tower lighthouse, 239–40
Chapel-le-Dale, 87
Chequers, 192, 200
Cholmley Estate, 205
Clapham, 76, 78, 79, 81, 82, 83, 109,
    112
Clapham Beck, 76, 78, 89
Clapham Gill, 79
Cleveland Hills, 153, 157
Cleveland Plain, 153
Cleveland Way, 153, 154, 161, 162,
    191, 192, 193, 200, 209, 211, 212,
    287–8
Cliff Ridge Wood, 154
Cloughton, 209
Coast-to-Coast Walk, 131, 289
Cod Beck, 193
Cook Monument, 153, 155–7; 156
Coverham Abbey, 105
Cowan Bridge, 275
Cowbar Nab, 163, 165; 164
Crina Bottom, 76, 79
Cross Keys Temperance Hotel, 37
Crummack Dale, 109, 111, 112

Dalby Forest, 147
Dales Way, 116, 117, 120, 289
Danes' Dyke, 25, 233, 235, 237
Danes' Graves, 237
Deep Dale, 223, 226
Derwent, River, 289
Derwent Way, 289
Devil's Arrows, 24
Devil's Dump, 208
Devonshire Estate, 117
Dick Delf Hill, 273
Doe, River, 57, 58, 59, 62
Doncaster, 28, 29
Dovedale Griff, 149

Earl Crag, 284
Earl's Scout, 284
Easby Abbey, 43, 44, 46
Easby Moor, 153
East Gill Force, 131
Ebor Way, 263, 265, 267, 289
Edale, 287
Edge, The, 124, 127

Elslack, 281, 284, 285
Elslack Moor, 281, 283
Embsay, 117
Esk, River, 183, 212, 213
Esk Dale, 204
Eskdale Way, 289
Esklets Cross, 185, 187
Esklets Farm, 183, 187

Falling Foss, 201, 204, 207–8
Falling Foss and Lilla Howe walk, 22,
    201–8; 206
Farndale, 187
Fat Betty (White Cross), 185, 187, 189;
    188
Fell Beck, 81, 82, 83
Filey, 26, 287, 288
Flamborough, 235, 239, 240; 241
Flamborough Head
    headland, 24, 25, 221, 233, 235, 237,
        239; 236
    walk, 21, 25, 233–41; 236, 238, 241
Flask Inn, 209
Force Gill, 84
Forest of Bowland, 83
Foss, River, 25, 246, 249
Foster Howes, 204, 207
Fountains Abbey
    walk, 19, 243, 254–62; 256, 258,261
    mentioned, 65, 73, 105, 124, 144
Fountains Fell, 73, 75, 284
Freeholders' Wood, 50, 53
Furness, 260
Fylingdales Moor, 204, 207

Gaping Gill, 76, 78, 81–3
Garsdale, 54, 67
Goathland
    village, 175, 177, 180, 289
    walk, 20, 174–80; 178
Gordale Beck, 93, 99
Gordale Scar, 34, 91, 93, 95, 97, 291;
    100
Gordale Scar and Malham Cove walk,
    21, 90–101; 92, 96, 100
Gouthwaite Reservoir, 127
Gragareth, 57
Grain Ings, 84

Great Ayton, 154, 155, 157
Green Dragon Inn, Hardraw, 63, 65, 68
Greenhow Hill, 34
Greenland's Howe, 207
Greensett Moss, 84
Greta, River, 59
Gribdale Gate, 153
Grinton, 133
Grosmont, 180
Gunnerside, 133
Gunnerside Gill, 135

Hambleton Drove Road, 192, 199
Hambleton Hills, 137, 138
Hardraw, 49, 63, 65, 67
Hardraw Force
   walk, 19, 54, 63–9; *66*
   waterfall, 63, 65, 68–9; *66*
Harrogate, 13, 243, 267
Hawes, 54, 63, 65, 67–8 *see also*
   Leyburn to Hawes Railway
Haworth
   Brontë Parsonage Museum, 271, 275, 277–8
   village, 271, 279
   walk, 21, 271–9; *274*, *276*
Haworth Moor, 277, 279, 288
Hawkswick 104
Haylands Bridge, 65
Headland Way, 233
Helmsley, 267, 287, 288, 289
High Lingrow, 162
High Scar, 211
High Scarcliff, 283
High Stone Dyke, 185
Hinderwell, 162, 166
Hole of Horcum, 179
Horton in Ribblesdale, 71, 73–4, 75, 290
Hovingham, 20, 243, 263–7; *266*
How Stean Gorge, 123, 125, 127, 128
   walk 22, 122–8; *126*
Howardian Hills, 289
Howdale Moor, 209
Howgill Fells, 39, 289
Hull, 28
Hull Pot, 73, 76

Humber Bridge, 288
Humberside, 288
Hunt Pot, 73, 75
Huntcliff, 26
Hunter's Sty, 186

Ickornshaw Moor, 284
Ilkley, 120, 267, 285, 289
In Moor, 123
Ingleborough
   peak, 25, 57, 58, 59, 71, 75, 76, 78, 83, 109, 284, 290; *80*
   walk to summit, 22, 76–83; *80*
Ingleborough Cave, 78, 81, 82, 112
Ingleborough Hall, 79, 109
Ingleby Greenhow, 173
Ingleton, 33, 57, 58, 59, 61, 76, 78, 79, 83 *see also* Ingleton Waterfalls
Ingleton Waterfalls, 19, 56–62; *60*
Janet's Foss, 91, 93, 94–5
Jervaulx Abbey, 55, 73, 260
John Cross, 203, 205
Jonathan Gill, 147
Jorvik, 27, 247, 253

Keld, 129, 132, 133
Kettle Ness, 161, 166, 179
Kettlewell, 103, 105, 107
Kilnsey Crag, 33, 105
Kirby Stephen, 37
Kirby Underdale, 231
Kirk Yetholm, 287
Kisdon Force, 131, 133, 135
Knaresborough, 24
Knipe Scar, 105, *106*

Lad Gill Hill, 131
Lady Chapel, 191, 195–6, 247–8
Lake District, 39, 120, 289, 293
Lambert Hag Wood, 143
Leyburn to Hawes Railway, 50, 54, 67
Lilla Howe, 27, 203, 205–7; *206*
Lilla Howe and Falling Foss walk, 22, 201–8; *206*
Lingrow Cliffs, 162
Lingrow Knowle, 165
Little Beck, 208

Little Ingleborough, 78 see also
    Ingleborough
Littondale, 103, 104, 105, 107
Littondale and Wharfedale walk, 20,
    102–7; 106
Lofthouse, 123, 125
Lothersdale, 283, 284
Low Dalby, 147
Low Staindale, 147
Low Wood, 147, 149
Lyke Wake Walk, 176, 181, 183, 192,
    199, 209, 290

Malham, 91, 94, 97, 98, 284, 291
Malham Beck, 93, 99
Malham Cove, 33–4, 91, 94, 98, 99,
    101, 107, 291; 92
Malham Cove and Gordale Scar walk,
    21, 90–101; 92, 96,100
Malham Tarn, 93, 98–9
Mallerstang, 39, 40
Mallyan Spout, 177, 179
Malton, 179
Margery Bradley Stone, 183, 185, 189
Marston Moor, 29, 243
Marton, 155
May Beck, 201, 203
Middlesbrough, 155, 173, 209
Middlesmoor, 123, 125, 128
Millington, 227, 229, 231–2
Millington Bottom, 229
Millington Dale, 20, 227–32, 288; 230
Milllington Pastures, 222, 229, 231
Minster Way, 227, 229, 231, 289
Moughton Scar, 111
Mount Grace Priory, 191, 192, 195,
    196; 197
Muker, 133
Mulgrave, 179

Needle Point, 149
Ness Point, 211
Newby Cote, 78
Newby Moss, 78
Newton Dale, 179
Newton Moor, 154
Nidd, River, 124, 125
Nidderdale, 34, 123, 125, 127–8; 126

Nidderdale Way, 123, 124, 127
Norber Erratics, 20, 108–13; 110
North Hush, 135
North Landing, 235, 240
North Wolds Walk, 227, 229, 231
North York Moors, 13, 15, 23–4, 27,
    30, 137–220, 221, 257, 287, 289,
    290, 293
Northallerton, 28, 49, 200, 243

Oak Dale, 192, 193; 198
Old Ralph Cross see Ralph Crosses
Old Wife's Trod 205
Osmotherley
    village, 191, 193, 195, 288; 194
    walk, 21, 190–200; 194, 197, 198
Ouse, River, 25, 247, 248, 249, 289, 290
Oxenhope Stoop Hill, 273

Park Scar, 104
Peak National Park, 269
Peak Steel, 211
Pecca Falls, 58, 61; 60
Pen-y-ghent
    peak, 33, 71, 73, 75, 109, 284, 290;
        72
    walk to summit, 21, 71–6; 72
Pendle Hill, 284
Penistone Hill, 271, 273, 275, 279
Pennine Way, 63, 93, 94, 129, 131, 136,
    273, 279, 283, 284–5, 287
Pennines, 13, 15, 30, 229, 269–85 see
    also Pennine Way
Pickering, 179, 180, 243
Pinhaw Beacon walk, 20, 280–5; 282
Ponden Hall, 279
Pontefract, 28
Porridge Stoop, 283, 284; 282
Port Mulgrave, 162, 165

Ralph Crosses, 185, 187,189; 184
Ransable Hill, 283
Ravenscar, 209, 211, 212, 219, 220, 290
    walk from Whitby to, 13, 22,
        209–22; 215, 216, 218
Ravenseat, 132, 133
Rawthey, River, 37
Redmire, 54

Ribble, River, 71
Ribble Valley, 284
Ribble Way, 289
Ribblehead Viaduct, 87–9; *88*
Ribblesdale, 33, 75, 83, 98
Ribchester, 285
Richmond, 13, 19, 28, 41–7, 135; *45*
Rievaulx
    Abbey, 141, 143–4, 146, 187, 287–8;
        142, 145
    Terrace, 141, 146
    village, 141, 143
    walk, 19, 140–6; *142, 145*
Ripon, 243
    Cathedral, 257, 262
Robbed Howe, 207
Robert's Seat, 132, 136
Robert's Seat House, 132, 136
Robin Hood's Bay, 209, 211, 217–9;
    216, 218
Robin Hood's Bay Road, 203
Robin Hood's Butts, 217
Robin Hood's Stone, 217
Robin Proctor's Scar, 111
Roseberry Topping
    peak, 137, 153, 154, 157–8, 193, 288;
        159
    walk, 20, 152–9; *156, 159*
Rosedale
    Abbey, 169, 171, 173, 189
    Railway, 170, 173, 185; *172*
    walk, 22, 168–73; *172*
Rosedale Cliffs, 162
Rudston, 24
Runswick Bay, 161, 162,165–6; *167*
Runswick Bay and Staithes walk, 20,
    160–7; *164, 167*
Rye, River, 141, 143
Ryedale, 141, 144, 146

St Agatha's Church, Richmond, 43,
    47
St Mary's Church, Studley Park, 257,
    262
St Mary's Church, Whitby, 211, 214
Saltburn, 287
Saltwick Nab, 211
Scar, The, 86

Scar House Reservoir, 123, 125 127,
    128; *126*
Scarborough, 209, 288
Scarth Nick, 191 ,192, 290
Scarth Wood Moor, 192
Sedburgh, 37, 39
Sedbusk, 65
Selwicks Bay, 235, 239–40; *238*
Semer Water, 98
Settle to Carlisle Railway, 54, 84, 86–9
Shap, 260
Shaw Gill Wood, 69
Shot Lathe, 133
Simon Seat, 284
Simonstone, 67
Skell, River, 255, 257, 259
Skipton, 120
Skirfare, River, 103, 104
Skirwith Quarry, 59
Slack Hill, 84
Snow Falls, 59, 62
South Landing, 233, 237, 240
Spurn Head, 243
Staithes, 155, 161, 163–5; *164*
Staithes and Runswick Bay walk, 20,
    160–7; *164, 167*
Stamford Bridge, 28, 289
Standard battlefield, 243
Startindale Gill, 131
Station Inn, 84
Stonesdale Beck, 132
Stonesdale Moor, 131, 135
Stony Leas, 203
Stony Marl Moor, 209
Stoupe Beck, 211, 212
Street Gate, 93, 98
Strid, The, 115, 116, 117, 119–20; *118*
Strid and Bolton Abbey walk, 21,
    114–21; *118*
Strid Wood, 117
Studley Park, 255, 257, 262; *256*
Swainby, 191
Swale, River, 41, 43, 131; *45*
Swaledale, 34, 129, 131, 133, 135
Swaledale and Tan Hill walk, 21,
    129–36; *134*
Swilla Glen, 58, 61
Sylvan Dale, 229

Tabular Hills, 137, 138
Tabular Hills Link, 288
Tan Gill, 132
Tan Hill, 34, 129, 131, 135–6
    Inn,129, 131, 135–6; *134*
Tan Hill and Swaledale walk, 21,
    129–36; *134*
Tees Valley, 137
Thixendale, 231
Thomas Gill, 132
Thornton Dale, 147
Thornton Force, 33, 58, 61–2
Thornton-in-Craven, 283
Thornwick Bay, 235, 239
Three Peaks
    Three Peaks Walk (challenge walk),
        74, 290
    walks to summits, 70–89; *72*, *80*, *88*
    mentioned, 16, 17
    see also Ingleborough; Pen-y-ghent;
        Whernside
Thwaite, 129, 133
Top Withins, 271, 273, 278–9; *276*
Tranlands Beck, 99
Trow Gill, 78, 82
Twiss, River, 57, 58, 59, 61

Upper Swaledale corpse road, 133
Ure, River, 49, 51, 53, 63, 65, 68, 290

Vale of Mowbray, 191
Vale of Pickering, 137, 179, 243, 289
Vale of York, 137, 229, 231, 243–67,
    289, 290
Valley of Desolation, 116
Viking Way, 288
Virosidum, 26

Wade's Causeway (Roman Road), 26,
    176, 179; *178*
Wainstones, 151
Warren Dale, 227
Water Sinks, 93, 99
Watlowes Dry Valley, 94, 99, 101
Wensley, 65
Wensleydale, 26, 33, 54, 55, 65
West Beck, 175, 176

Westerdale, 22, 181, 186, 187
Westerdale Moor 181–9; *184*, *188*
Wharfe, River, 103, 105, 115, 116, 119
Wharfedale, 98, 103, 104, 105
Wharfedale and Littondale walk, 20,
    102–7; *106*
Wharram le Street, 223
Wharram Percy
    medieval village, 222, 223, 226, 288;
        225
    walk, 19, 223–6; *225*
Wheeldale Moor, 26, 179
Whernside
    peak, 57, 58, 59, 71, 75, 76, 84, 86,
        89, 284, 290; *88*
    walk to summit, 72, 84 9; *88*
Whinstone Ridge, 204
Whitby
    Abbey, 137, 205, 211, 214, 217, 219
    features of interest, 211, 212–7; *215*
    Whitby to Pickering Railway, 177,
        179–80
    Whitby to Ravenscar walk, 13, 22,
        209–22; *215*, *216*, *218*
    mentioned, 149, 155, 157, 166, 173,
        175, 179, 201, 289
White Cross (Fat Betty), 185, 187, 189;
    188
Wild Boar Fell, 40
Wolds Way, 223, 227, 229, 231, 288
Wrack Hills, 162

Yore Mill, 49, 51, 55
Yoredale Way, 290
York
    Castle, 247, 253
    history, 25–6, 27, 28, 29
    Jorvik, 27, 247, 253
    Minster, 205, 231, 245–6, 249–51;
        250
    The Shambles, 246, 251; *252*
    walk around, 19, 243, 244–53; *250*,
        252
    mentioned, 13, 257, 267, 289, 290
Yorkshire Dales, 13, 15, 33–136, 138,
    139, 269, 287, 289, 290, 293
Yorkshire Wolds, 13, 25, 30, 221–41
Young Ralph Cross *see* Ralph Crosses